WAS THERE A PEPSI GENERATION BEFORE PEPSI DISCOVERED IT?

Youth-Based Segmentation in Marketing

Stanley C. Hollander
Richard Germain
Foreword by Richard S. Tedlow, Harvard University

Published by NTC Business Books in Association with
the American Marketing Association

AMERICAN
MARKETING
ASSOCIATION

NTC Business Books
NTC a division of *NTC Publishing Group* • Lincolnwood, Illinois USA

The publisher thanks all the companies who contributed advertisements
and gave permission for these to be reproduced in this book. Every
effort was made to contact all copyright holders. If there has been
any oversight, we would be pleased to update our information
when the book is reprinted.

Published in conjunction with the American Marketing Association,
250 South Wacker Drive, Chicago, Illinois, 60606.

Cataloging-in-publication data is available from the Library of Congress.

1993 Printing

Published by NTC Business Books, a division of NTC Publishing Group
4255 West Touhy Avenue
Lincolnwood (Chicago), Illinois 60646-1975, U.S.A.
3 4 5 6 7 8 9 BC 9 8 7 6 5 4 3 2

To Selma D. J. Hollander

Innumerable businesses recognize the existence of market contours by putting out their products in two or more grades, retaining as much of the essential utility or style as is compatible with the reduction in price which will bring the various grades within the reach of prospects on various economic planes. This is an accepted practice among manufacturers of clothing for men and women, watches, talking machines, cameras, hand tools, and a long list of other products having general appeal

(SHAW 1916, p.228-9).

CONTENTS

F O R E W O R D

This study is a remarkable piece of work that unites the history of marketing practice with the current concerns of today's marketing practitioner. As modern marketing seems to be moving forward with ever increasing speed into what can only be described as "hyper-segmentation", Stanley C. Hollander, the dean of marketing historians, and Richard Germain take a look back. Focusing specifically on the youth segment, they ask how and why did this set of customers come to be recognized as a distinct group with its own characteristics, desires, and antipathies. How was this market nurtured? Who served it most effectively and why?

Drawing on a remarkable range of primary and secondary sources (including an occasional personal reminiscence), Hollander and Germain have written what is probably the best history of a particular market segment now available. Their analysis poses some urgent questions to the modern marketer:

- To what extent did youth marketing develop because "youth" constituted a "natural" market segment?
- If the youth market is an example of a natural segment, are there other natural segments today just waiting to be recognized and served by the perspicacious marketer?
- How did the youth market change over time?
- To what extent was the youth market not natural but rather a segmentation category "created" by marketers?
- If this segment could be so successfully created, what segments can be created in the future?

The research of Hollander and Germain will stimulate both intellectual reflection and action-oriented thinking about these questions.

In addition, this book is written in a lively and engaging fashion all too rarely found in studies of marketing history or of business history in general, for that matter. It is difficult not to chuckle, for example, about the university president who ''once described his college student daughter as being at that awkward age where she didn't know what wine to serve with the Twinkies. . . .''

Marketing is work, but it is also fun. Hollander and Germain capture both these aspects of it.

The reader will find that the authors take issue with my own work at a number of points. Indeed, they conclude by saying that ''The answer to the question 'Was there a Pepsi Generation before Pepsi discovered it?' is *yes*.'' My own answer would be ''Yes and no.''

But such disagreements are to be expected and even welcomed. The point is that through voluminous research which they wear very lightly, Hollander and Germain have pushed forward our understanding of how modern marketing evolved and—both explicitly and by implication—have provided us with food for thought about the future.

RICHARD S. TEDLOW
Harvard Business School

ACKNOWLEDGMENTS

The completion of this book would have been impossible without the much appreciated help of a number of people. We thank the following individuals, listed alphabetically, for providing us with material: Alexander Angelle, Lieutenant Colonel, Chief of Public Affairs, U.S. Army, Recruiting Services; Kimberly Barta, The American Advertising Museum; Joyce E. Bryant, Vice President of Consumer Affairs, Household International; Cynthia D'Angelo, Educational Director at the National Association of College Book Stores; Professor Karen Gillespie, School of Education, New York University and past director of its Institute of Retail Management; Karen Goldblatt, Director of Research, Muzak; Lyle E. Goss, retired manager of the University of Washington bookstore and past President of the National Association of College Stores; Alfreda L. Irwin, Historian-in-Residence, Chatauqua Historical Collection; Robert Kahn of Lafayette, California; Professor Alan Lloyd, former official of the Business Education Association; Professor Richard W. Pollay, Curator, The History of Advertising Archives; Kimberly A. Rich, Curator, Hallmark Historical Collection of Hallmark Cards, Inc.; H. R. Sinruer, Archival Consultant, B'Nai Brith; and Les Stegh, Archivist, Deere & Company.

We would also like to thank Professors Roger Dickenson, Morris L. Mayer, and Richard S. Tedlow, and one individual who chose to remain anonymous, for carefully providing feedback on the early draft manuscripts for the book. Our appreciation also extends to Dean J. Barry Mason, University of Alabama. We thank Francesca Van Gorp of the American Marketing Association and Jane Lott of Michigan State University for their patience through the revision process. Michigan State University has nurtured our work on this project over the past several years, and we are grateful to the MSU All-University Research Fund, to Dean Richard Lewis of the Eli Broad Graduate School of Management, and to Chairperson Robert Mason of the Marketing and Transportation Department for their support. We also appreciate the help that Dean Robert L. Sandmeyer and Marketing Chairpersons Stephen Miller and Lee Manzer of Oklahoma State University, College of Business Administration, have given us. Last, but not least, we thank Anne Knudsen and Karen Shaw of NTC Business Books for their careful and detailed editing of the manuscript. Of course, any errors, omissions, or mistakes remain the responsibility of the authors.

INTRODUCTION

Hebe, Juventus to the Romans, was the Greek goddess of youth and cup bearer to the other gods. In the pages that follow, we intend to show how late 19th century and early 20th century marketers used her and myriad other images to induce the rest of the population to drink from the cup of youthfulness, and how today's marketers continue to promote the appeal of youth.

Drinking from the cup involves two types of youth marketing. The first is marketing to youth—that is, the conscious segmentation of the market on the basis of age. The second type of youth marketing involves injecting of youthfulness into products and services—that is, youthfulness marketing.

✳ Marketing to youth is a focal point of current marketers' interest for three principle reasons. First, it is a legitimate market of considerable size in its own right (Gage 1982; Hulin-Sakin 1982). The numbers of youth have fluctuated across time reflecting broad-based demographic shifts, and this has shifted marketers' emphasis. The relative importance of the youth segment increased during the 1960s, and may, as a result of population aging, decrease during the 1990s. But it is and will remain a significant segment that marketers find difficult to ignore.

Second, many marketers believe youth form purchasing patterns that extend far into their lifetime (Adler 1987; Moschis 1987). A logical extension of this view is *cohort theory* (Crosby, Gill and Lee 1984). Oversimplifying at this point, cohort theory holds that experiences during formative years permanently modify future behavior. Thus all (or the great majority) who were young in the Depression years of the 1930s could be expected to have become different adults than those who were young in the 1920s, the 1960s, or 1990s.

One study, sponsored by DuPont, identified ten cohort groups (*Stores* 1989). Due to the 1930 Depression, those born between 1910 and 1919, World War I Babies, "remain cautious about spending." Those born between 1946 and 1950, Mature Boomers, tend to be "ambivalent toward materialism," while those born between 1958 and 1964, Mature Busters, tend to focus on "making money and spending it on themselves" (p. 36). Mature boomers formed part of the youth segment during the 1960–70s' youth movement, and Mature Busters formed part of the more conservative and materialistic youth segment during the 1980s "Me Generation."

Other studies have examined consumers' current preferences dependent on behavior, experiences, or preferences during their formative transition from adolescence to adulthood. One study reported that 30 percent of females between the ages of 20 and 24 still use the first cosmetic brand tried as teenagers (Fannis 1984). Regardless of current age, popular music heard at the age of 24 remains the most-liked popular music through an individual's lifetime (Holbrook and Schlinder 1989). The same may hold for clothes and furniture. In nonprofit institutions, bonds fostered during youth may be translated in later years into financial and moral support and volunteerism (e.g., alumni activities).

Third, youth influence the purchasing behavior and decision-making processes of younger and older individuals and of family members (Loudon and Della Bitta 1984; Stern 1984; *Stores* 1988). The increasing number of two-working-parent families may further enhance the effect of youth on family purchasing behavior. Teenagers now spend more time doing the family food shopping than their parents did during their youth (Hauser 1986; Yorovich 1982). The collegiate youth market is also important: it "has influence all out of proportion to its size because it is a great endorser of innovative products and ideas" (Mihaly 1984, p. 48).

Moreover, marketers have learned that youthfulness is an appeal to which many older (adult) and younger (children) consumers often respond. They have used this appeal to sell automobiles, apparel, shoes, food, exercise equipment and sporting goods, health and beauty aids, and all sorts of other goods and services. This raises a problem when youthfulness appeals are used to promote controversial products such as cigarettes and alcohol. Critics claim that such appeals are used to draw new young consumers into the market. The advertisers claim that they are simply using a standard mechanism to reach a somewhat vulnerable mature market.

This book traces the development of both types of youth marketing in the United States. Growing gradually during the late 19th century, and more noticeably during the 20th century, marketing to youth and youthfulness marketing were firmly established practices by the beginning of World War II.

Chapter 1 set the stage for the study. Richard Tedlow's (1990) three phases of segmentation are reviewed, and youthfulness marketing is examined in more detail. In Chapter 1, we also explore problems associated with defining youth, and with distinguishing between segmention and product diversification. The data upon which the book is based are discussed in this chapter.

Chapter 2 returns to the issue of the importance of the youth market. In this case, the emphasis is on the 1880–1940 time period.

Chapters 3, 4, and 5 describe how youth marketers adjusted promotion, price and distribution, and product. Many examples of youth marketing are presented in this chapter.

Chapter 6 focuses on how nonprofit institutions including colleges, churches, and the military cultivated youth markets.

Chapter 7 discusses the findings and presents implications of the previous chapters. In it, we discuss attention devoted to youth, youth movements, the distinction between cohort theory and youth influence, the rise of the United States consumer culture, the ease and difficulty of youth marketing, the distinction between product differentiation and segmentation, similarities and differences between marketing to youth and marketing to the elderly, and, finally, adoption of youth marketing strategies.

The Study of Youth Marketing

I n his book, *New and Improved: The Story of Mass Marketing in America,* Richard Tedlow (1990), professor of business history at Harvard University and former editor of the *Business History Review,* divides American marketing into three phases, which he also calls the three phases of market segmentation. In accordance with the business historical tradition developed at Harvard by N.S.B. Gras (Gras and Larson 1939) and continued by many American business historians, Tedlow (1990) organizes his study of market segmentation development around four industry (corporate conflict) case histories.

- Phase I, fragmentation, involved small producers selling low volume output at high margins to restricted markets.

It was a period of geographic segmentation enforced by the absence of adequate transportation and communication infrastructures. This period ended around 1880.

- Phase II, unification, was marked by the development, promotion, and exploitation of mass markets. It featured large volumes, scale economies, low prices, and the dominance of national brands.

- Phase III, segmentation, saw the market large enough to support relatively economical production of specialized outputs that catered to demographic and psychographic consumer segments. Scale economies, value-based rather than cost-based pricing, high volume, and demographic and psychographic segmentation characterize this phase.

Tedlow observed that the adoption of the three phases of segmentation did not occur contemporaneously in all industries. Ford's Model T was an outcome of Phase II unification. It was mass produced in one color only, distributed nationally, priced to fit low- and middle-class pocketbooks, and suitable, or so Ford thought, for the entire market. General Motors displaced Ford during the 1920s and 1930s by adopting a Phase III segmentation strategy. Its vehicles came in many colors, sizes, and prices, and thus appealed to various specialized market segments. Similarly, Coca-Cola, according to Tedlow, used Phase II unification during the same time period, and it was not until the 1960s when Pepsi-Cola sought the youth market that Phase III segmentation was applied to the soft drink industry.

Tedlow might well have added a fourth phase to his list: segment creation or positioning. He sees the Pepsi-Cola ''Pepsi Generation'' youth appeal strategy as not only a recognition of a distinct demographic segment (although it was in part that), but as the creation of a group of consumers who wanted to feel or seem young. He says (p.372) ''there was no such thing as the Pepsi

Generation until Pepsi created it.'' That is, of course, a rhetorical flourish in a highly readable, but serious work in marketing history. We have no intention here of quibbling over a phrase. Rather, in accordance with Tedlow's point that phases have emerged at different times in different industries (and one might add not necessarily in I, II, III, IV sequence), we want to explore the question of whether a substantial amount of *youth segmentation* occurred before 1940.

Konrad (1990) observed, in a review of Tedlow (1990) and *Satisfaction Guaranteed: The Making of the American Mass Market* (Strasser 1989), that the fundamental impression created by the two books is that few ''modern'' marketing practices are really modern. Similar positions have been taken by Hollander (1986), Fullerton (1988), and Pollay (1985). Fullerton (1985) also noted that early segmentation existed in the German book trade of the 19th century.

Market segmentation can be defined as ''the act of dividing a market into distinct and meaningful groups of buyers who might merit separate products and/or marketing mixes'' (Kotler 1980, p.294). We added a fourth phase to Tedlow's (1990) original three, Phase IV segmentation, and labeled it positioning or segment creation. It is an active effort to foster in consumers, or extant consumer segments, an image of what they ought to be. Part of that image, of course, includes consumption of the product. Ideally, ''the implicit goal of market segmentation [and segment creation] for a business firm is to increase profit over what it would be without segmentation'' (Rudelius, Walton, and Cross 1987, p.385).

Historical analysis of market segmentation can take several forms. An attempt to measure all segmentation by all companies over an extensive time range would be both physically and economically impossible. Conceivably, one might attempt to observe how much segmentation appeared to exist at any one point in time. A second alternative is to pursue case histories of particular companies or industries as Tedlow did. The third alternative is to select one particular form of segmentation and pursue it over a considerable period of time. That has been our choice.

With the exception of work in oral history, historical research is essentially an unintrusive approach complicated by the vagaries and difficulties of data availability. It does not lend itself to easy quantification. Instead, like other unintrusive measures, it must rely upon triangulation or the use of a variety of approaches for verification or contradiction. In this study, we sought evidence of whether American marketers used one demographic segmentation variable, *age,* and, in particular, whether they targeted *youth* (roughly the 15–24 year age group), prior to World War II.

Youth as Our Variable

The choice of the youth category was entirely external to the examination of segmentation. It resulted from an attempt by the International Commission on the History of Social Movements and Social Structures. The commission is partially continual and partially an ad hoc academic group that correlates its activities with those of International Economic History Association. During the late 1980s, the commission's American section encouraged interdisciplinary work concerning youth in society.

The choice of other groups might have yielded more or less evidence of segmentation. We strongly suspect that gender segmentation was more common than age segmentation in the period under review, and that age segmentation on the basis of child versus adult would have yielded sharper distinctions than the intermediate age bracket did. On the other hand, since persons of other ages have sometimes seen some fantasized version of ''youthfulness'' or ''youngness'' as a desirable state, choice of youth for analysis may furnish some unusual examples of psychographic segmentation and appeals to those who wanted to appear or feel youthful.

Defining Youth

Defining youth involves two problems. First is whether youth existed in any widespread sense before very recent times. Many historically minded researchers doubt whether the phenomenon of youth itself existed until very modern times. They argue (for example Hawes and Hines 1985) that the great majority of Americans went directly from childhood to working adulthood until very recently. A British historian, Plumb, in a book that became the stimulus for much modern consumer behavior history (McKendrick, Brewer, and Plumb 1982), held that until recently even childhood was a rarity, for people passed from infant directly to laborer.

While Hawes and Hines (1985) and Plumb (McKendrick, Brewer, and Plumb 1982) have argued that youth is a recent aspect of our society, we join the many other social historians (Fass 1977; Fox 1977; Gillis 1974) who believe youth (whether labeled so or not) has long been an important phenomenon. Minimum voting and office-holding ages, maximum military draft age and the creation of youth-oriented organizations such as the YWCA, YMCA, and the junior branches of many fraternal and social organizations are only a few examples of the ways in which society distinguished between youth and full maturity, even for the employed population.

The second definitional problem concerns measuring the borders of youth. Many sociologists (Taylor 1988) and marketers (Gilbert 1957; Helitzer and Heyel 1970; Moschis 1987) use determinant age brackets such as 15 to 24 to define youth, pre-adulthood, young adulthood, or some other descriptor of the relevant age group. In contrast, the American participants in the International Commission's work wanted to center on dependent adolescence and older youth: in particular, those attending post secondary educational institutions.

In general, we opted for the chronological characterization because emancipated and dependent youth are subject to many of the same legal restrictions, the same needs, and the same biological and, consequently, psychobiological changes. Both constitute important markets. Emancipated youth may well be involved in household establishment and family formation. They also often wish to emulate collegiate or dependent youth who, ironically, nurture desires for independence.

Thus, for the purpose of market segmentation, the concept of *youth* possesses considerable ambiguity and variability of chronological age limits. Yet it can have considerable meaning for the individual consumer and, more importantly in our context, for the marketer.

For the modern North American consumer, McCracken (1986, p.72), an historically-minded cultural sociologist, argues that such cultural categories as age are "elective." The individual has some considerable ability to determine position.

> First, they [categories of person] possess an indeterminacy that is not normally evident in other ethnographic circumstances. For instance, cultural categories of person are marked by a persistent and striking lack of clarity, as are cultural categories of age. Second, they possess an apparent "elective" quality. Devoted as it is to the freedom of the individual, contemporary North American society permits its members to declare at their own discretion the cultural categories they presently occupy. Exercising this freedom, teenagers declare themselves adults, members of the working class declare themselves middle class, the old declare themselves young, and so on. Category membership, which in most cultures is more strictly specified and policed, is in our own society much more a matter of individual choice. In our culture, individuals are to a great extent what they claim to be, even when these claims are by some sober sociological reckoning, implausible.

There may or may not have been more rigidity in early 20th century society. Yet then, as now, adolescents and post-adolescents exhibited considerable variation in independence, maturity, and responsibility. Cohorts did not move through life in lockstep. So while we are mainly thinking of 15- to 24-year-olds as our archetypes, we must recognize that some people were almost born, certainly reared, as "little old men and women." Others "never grew up."

More significantly, segmentation is at least partly determined by the needs of segmenters. Marketers can see the consumer market as consisting of infants–adults, infants–children–adults, or infants–children–youth–adults, with possible further subdivision and certainly with the addition of senior adult categories. A manufacturer of college insignia apparel would want to draw the age divisions at a different point than a manufacturer of *starter* household furniture or appliances. The common thread, and the point that we wish to examine in this book, is that both may see the existence of markets between childhood and conventional full adulthood.

OUR RESOURCES

The literature used for this book came from archives,[1] marketing trade and consumer periodicals published at various times during the first half of the 20th century, a number of marketing and consumer economics texts, and from a rapidly growing body of retrospective social history studies.

Exhibits 2-1, 3-1, and 3-3 list 1880–1940 youth marketing literature citations (archival, consumer advertising, and retrospective sources are not listed). Like Tedlow (1990), we were unable to locate the word "positioning" in any of the articles. A library administrator named Joseph Wheeler (1935) used the word "segment" and Giles (1922, p.60) used the word "target" as follows: "Youth . . . should be the bull's-eye of your advertising target." Words or phrases like "market" (Gridley 1923; *Sales Management*

---

1. The primary archive was the Warshaw Collection of American Business Ephemera, Collection 60, Center for Advertising History, Center for Archival Research, National Museum for American History, Smithsonian Institution, Washington D.C. The School and College, Dry Goods and Menswear holdings were examined.

1934), "public" (Fallows 1901; Titus 1935), and "college market" (Burns 1926; Dumont 1929; George 1929) were commonly used to describe the population subgroup consisting of youth or students. Whether these differences indicate shifting terminology or practice is critical to our examination; however, the reviewed articles' contents suggest a variation in terminology rather than substance from modern concepts of segmentation.

The citations listed in Exhibits 2-1, 3-1 and 3-3 primarily come from trade publications such as *Printers' Ink, Sales Management*, and *Printers' Ink Monthly. Printers' Ink,* the leading American advertising and marketing trade publication during the late 19th and the first half of the 20th century, was initially published in 1888. By the beginning of World War II, many well-known marketing scholars (Percival White, Albert Haring) and business practitioners (Alfred Sloan) had contributed articles.

Three types of authors listed in Exhibits 2-1, 3-1, and 3-3 were identified. First, some were editorial staff members (Dickinson 1919), business commentators or unidentified contributors. Second, some were business practitioners including: Ellison (1934), advertising manager of Brunswick–Balke–Colander Co. (a maker of billiard tables); Hall (*Printers' Ink* 1915c), advertising manager of Alpha Portland Cement Company; and Downs (*Printers' Ink* 1936), president of the Illinois Central System, a railroad. Lastly, some writers were academicians (Russell 1926; Donnell 1940; Jacobson 1928).

One word of caution. The sensitive reader may detect some elements of chauvinism underlying some of our examples, but hopefully not our observations. We are trying to depict marketing practices in an era that was (by modern standards) quite chauvinistic. In her history of 1920s American youth, Paula Fass (1977), observes that she, along with other historians, concentrated on white, urban, middle-class collegiate youth. The same could be said for many of the people who wrote on the youth market for the trade press. Whether this is due to the fact that their children and their friends' children belonged to that category, and so were most familiar with it, or whether it was that the collegiate youth were indeed the pacesetters for all others, may be a question, but the result is relatively less attention to immigrant, minority, working-class, and non-academic youth.

Product Diversity

A slight digression concerned with product proliferation is in order at this point. We know that by the 1910s, manufacturers were producing an enormous variety of items and models within a great many product categories. The variations existed both between in-dividual sellers and within those sellers' lines. We know of this because of the efforts at product line simplification that were a part of World War I efficiency efforts (Hudson 1928; McCullough 1928). Product proliferation resumed after the war and ultimately became the target for a major standardization campaign spear-headed by Herbert Hoover during his tenure as Secretary of Com-merce. Proliferation dominated both consumer and industrial mar-kets. For instance, manufacturers of a mundane item like cotton work gloves were offering some 700 varieties (Hollander 1984).

This drive toward product line proliferation derived from many sources. Part of it was probably an attempt to escape direct product comparisons and, hence, lessen direct price competition between rival producers. Some of it was probably an attempt to retain monopolies on consumable supplies or specialized machines and instruments. One can draw the distinction between making a variety of items in response to both competitive and demand forces, on the one hand, and segmentation, on the other, in that segmenta-tion essentially involves regarding a market as being composed of identifiable subgroups who should be the focus of specialized marketing mixes. But the distinction is very tenuous, and prolifera-tion may well show an attempt to "please every customer's taste" which comes very close to catering to "every market segment." The point being that product diversity is conceptually at odds with all types of segmentation—marketing to youth being one of them.

A History of Marketing to Youth: 1880–1940

Exhibit 2.1 on the following page lists 1880–1940 citations that discuss the importance of the youth market. The three reasons described (youth as a legitimate market, youth as future consumers, and youth influence) are discussed in the sections that follow.

YOUTH AS A LEGITIMATE MARKET

Each author listed in Exhibit 2.1 presented empirical size and spending estimates for youth or a youth subsegment. Youth mar-

EXHIBIT 2.1
Literature summary: Why sell to youth (1880–1940)

Topic	Selected citations (alphabetical order)

Youth as a Legitimate Market

Youth market size	Allen 1933; Bradbury 1933; Grumbine 1934; Mathes 1933; *Printers' Ink* 1933
College market size	Lewis 1904; George 1929, North 1929; *Printers' Ink* 1915c; Russell 1926; *Sales Management* 1934
Youth market spending	Coutant and Smith 1938; Ellison 1934; *Photoplay Magazine* 1922
College market spending	Kuenstler 1940; Lewis 1904; North 1929; *Sales Management* 1933, 1934; Yocum 1934

Youth as Future Consumers

Allen 1933; Baird 1931; Coutant and Smith 1938; Dickinson 1932; Larned 1927; Mathes 1933; North 1929; Palmer and Schlink 1934; *Photoplay Magazine* 1922; *Printers' Ink* 1915c, 1924, 1935; Russell 1926; *Sales Management* 1934; Shepard 1935; Steglar 1938; Talbot 1937

Youth Influence

On family	Giles 1922; Muller 1931; *Photoplay Magazine* 1922; Wirth 1928
On other age groups	Cobb 1921; Erbes 1937; Giles 1922; Larned 1927; Mathes 1933; Nystrom 1928; Russell 1926

keting commentators, frequently relying on census data, noted during the early 1930s that two and a half million people became 16 each year (Allen 1933), six million individuals became 23 or 24 each year (Mathes 1933), and eleven million people were between the ages of 14 and 18 (Grumbine 1934).

Budget studies conducted during the early part of the 20th century (Nystrom 1929, p.338–41) revealed that daughters over the age of 15 consumed the highest proportion of the family clothing budget, regardless of total family income. Sons over the age of 15 typically consumed the next highest proportion of the family clothing budget. Differences were recognized in tastes and needs between, for example, fathers and sons. "The young men over 15 expend larger amounts for dress-up and sports purposes while fathers spend more for working clothes of all kinds" (Nystrom 1929, p.339).

In 1922, *Photoplay Magazine* sponsored a study conducted by Barton, Durstine and Osborn (now called BBDO) that examined age-related purchasing. The existence of such a study demonstrates that empirical research was used to examine age-based purchasing habits. Retailers were asked to estimate the proportion of purchases within their line of business made by each of four age groups. The selection of product categories included in the study probably was motivated by the desire to demonstrate the importance of the youth market. The magazine undoubtedly used the results summarized in the booklet as part of a soft sell campaign to attract advertisers.

The major findings of the study are reproduced in Table 2.1 (*Photoplay Magazine* 1922, p.17). In the upper portion of Table 2.1 are shown means estimated across sampled retailers. To provide a sense of relative purchasing behavior, census estimates of the proportion of the 1920 U.S. population in each age category are provided in the lowermost row in Table 2.1. For example, while retailers estimated that 48 percent of all hosiery purchases were made by the 18–30 age group, the 18–30 age category accounted for only 23 percent of the 1920 U.S. population. In general, youth (18–30) purchased the greatest amount relative to their actual numbers, followed by the 30–45 age group. The elder age category (over 45) and children (under 18) apparently purchased the least

TABLE 2.1

Summary of *Photoplay Magazine* research (1922)

Product	Proportions (%) of purchases made by each age category			
	Under 18	18–30	30–44	Over 44
Ready-to-wear	16	37	29	18
Dress goods	18	37	31	14
Hosiery	17	48	24	11
Underwear	16	45	26	13
Furniture	3	40	36	21
Rugs	2	42	37	19
Draperies	3	42	36	19
Phonographs and records	14	48	34	15
Wood instruments	26	48	18	8
Pianos	2	36	43	19
Percent of 1920 U.S. population	37%	23%	19%	21%

Sources:
1. Age-related purchasing habits from *Photoplay Magazine* (1922), *The Age Factor in Selling and Advertising*, New York: *Photoplay Magazine*.
2. U.S. population estimates from the *Fourteenth Census of the United States, Vol. II* (1920, p.162).

Notes:
Photoplay Magazine reported on the results of a study conducted by Barton, Durstine & Osborn (now called BBDO). Retail merchants in Buffalo, Hartford, Providence, Wilkes-Barre, PA, Easton, PA, Dunkirk, NY, and Natick, MA were asked what proportion of sales were accounted for by each age group. The proportions are, therefore, mean values across retail respondents. The number of sampled retailers varied with the product category. For example, for ready-to-wear, n = 37; for rugs, n = 26; and for phonographs and records, n = 36.

amount of the ten products relative to their share of the 1920 U.S. population.

In spite of the incongruity between *Photoplay Magazine*'s (1922) definition of youth (18–30) and ours (15–24), *Photoplay*'s research supports the notion that age and purchase habits for certain product categories are *not* independent. Of course, this analysis should be considered in light of the earlier mentioned caveat concerning how the product categories may have been selected as part of their own campaign to attract advertisers.

Albert T. Poffenberger, a noted professor of psychology and advertising educator at Columbia University, devoted an entire chapter in a 1925 book to *group* differences (age, gender, occupation). He commented at length on the *Photoplay Magazine* (1922) study, and observed:

> There is the feeling that a greater gap than ever existed before has been created between the mature and the young, and that young people not only rule the market as far as their own purchases are concerned, but they have a powerful influence upon all family purchases. . . . The young are radicals in the market, while the mature are conservatives. The resistance to new ideas to be met in the young is less than in the old, hence the wide-spread appeal to the young in current advertising (p.584).

With respect to the collegiate youth, *Sales Management* (1934) described the results of an empirical study of 1,000 youth from ten universities. Detailed figures were given for purchases and brand preferences of cigarettes, pens, autos, typewriters, soap, and watches. Yocum (1934) studied the buying habits of youth attending The Ohio State University.

A study of Harvard University students, a male institution during the 1920s, revealed that each annually purchased 6–8 shirts, 8 neckties, 6 pairs of underwear, 12 handkerchiefs, 12 pairs of socks, 2 pairs of suspenders, and 3 pairs of shoes. Among the possessions of 35 student residents were 5 banjos, 3 ukuleles, 2 pianos, and 31 typewriters. All 35 students had phonographs, and 28 had engraved stationery. It was also estimated that 85 percent of the Harvard student population smoked cigarettes (North 1929). Female students attending the University of Pennsylvania annually purchased 7 dresses, 5 sweaters, 3 skirts, 1 coat, 3 hats, 4 pairs of shoes, 25 pairs of hosiery, 12 lingerie items, 4 pairs of gloves, and 3 purses (Kuenstler 1940).

These figures may or may not have been representative of total college student spending. Both Harvard and Pennsylvania were atypical in being residential, urban, elitist, Ivy League institutions with some receptivity to co-education either within their own student body or through a nearby (Pennsylvania) or an adjacent female institution (Radcliffe). Thus, those schools may have been somewhat more dressy than their more rural or their more proletarian counterparts. More importantly, the studies show that researchers were documenting college student purchasing behavior. More generally, we can note that White (1927) felt that age-based segmentation could be used for the purpose of "planning future sales" (p.158).

Youth as Future Consumers

The importance of youth as future consumers was frequently mentioned (Allen 1933; Baird 1931; Larned 1927; Mathes 1933; Russell 1926; Steglar 1938; Talbot 1937) and is highlighted by the following quotations.

> . . . the need for recognizing the student as an embryonic buyer, and of molding him, while yet in college, along such lines as will later prove productive from the standpoint of future business (*Printers' Ink* 1915c, p.10).

> If I were the manufacturer of notions, I certainly would appeal to the young women of seventeen or eighteen to twenty-six to twenty-seven years, when she is forming the buying habits of a lifetime. Once these younger women learn an advertised brand and are satisfied with the product, they continue to ask for it by name (Helen Murphy, notions buyer for Gimbel Brothers, New York: quoted in *Photoplay Magazine* 1922, p.21).

> Advertising to younger people, to the customers of tomorrow, has established itself as a strong and tried merchandising principle (*Printers' Ink* 1924, p.124).

College men . . . are so valuable a present and *potential* market for certain types of staples and luxuries that many an advertising campaign includes copy prepared especially for them [emphasis supplied] (*Sales Management* 1934, p.506).

Most of us believe firmly in the importance of advertising to the younger families who are not only more responsive buyers of nationally advertised goods, but are at an age when the habit patterns being formed will follow them through their life (Coutant and Smith 1938, p.31).

In response to college promotional efforts by John Wanamaker, Brooks Brothers, and De Pina, important Philadelphia and New York clothing stores, Shepard (1935, p.32) stated that the advertiser ''will catch his prospect while buying habits are being formed.'' Concern with future buying habits of collegiate youth in particular may stem from their higher than average expected income stream. ''Here, concentrated and easily reached through legitimate means, is a part of our population which will some day be the most influential, from the standpoints of both buying power and prestige'' (North 1929, p.25).

Youth Influence

The early 20th century marketing literature on children contained many references to how children influence family purchasing behavior.

Adults listen carefully to youngster's preferences when buying anything for personal or family use (Muller 1931, p.57).

Children not only influence the buying decisions of parents, but they also have a magic way of growing up and becoming consumers themselves (Duncan 1923, p.36).

The child's influence is threefold. First, the boy or girl are in
themselves markets for certain products: toys, candies, clothes,
etc. Second, the child can have a definite indirect influence on
the sale of products for adult use. Third, the child of today becomes the buyer of tomorrow (Gridley 1923, p.31).

Children may have gone even farther and virtually dictated the
choice of residence location for their parents. Wirth (1928, p.246)
points out that in an upwardly mobile society, the children of
immigrants generally seek to move from the slum area first settled
by their parents. He cites (p.240), as typical, the story of a Jewish
immigrant retailer, comfortably ensconced in Chicago's near-
westside ghetto slum until his law school student son urged a move
to a more prestigious Lawrencedale district, which would more
favorably impress the son's snobbish friends. Wirth goes on to say:

In most instances it is the children who discover the ghetto for
their parents [i.e., recognize its circumscribed nature]. They go
to school; they work in the stores and offices in the loop; they
make friends; they go to dances and the girls are seen home by
escorts; they are mobile, and the world of the ghetto begins to
shrink, then to bore, and finally to disgust . . . sometimes parents
who feel at home because they have never been outside, resist
for a time, but then family conflicts arise that make life intolera-
ble. They eventually yield, and the exodus begins (p.243).

The aspirational nature of consumption, and particularly its
effect on the matrimonial market, was a common theme in American literature for a long time. Gordon and McArthur (1985) discussed this and drew by way of illustration on a story written by
Mary Terhune (1871), in which a young working-class couple is
distinguished from their colleagues by refined taste in living style
and furnishings. The husband prospers and the wife ultimately
uses her skill as a consumer to house and dress her daughter in a
way that facilitates a marriage with a scion of one of the town's
leading families. Although the mother does not achieve acceptability in her inlaws' circle, her daughter can now move there easily

because of the style and taste that she has absorbed. We have not yet discovered any evidence of the use of this appeal on the part of home furnishings and clothing manufacturers and retailers, but suspect that it was often subtly suggested by dressmakers, upholsterers, and other furniture suppliers.

According to Bailey (1988), a historian of 20th century courtship and dating, the switch in courtship practices from formal calls in the home to dating took place, at least in the middle class, during the 1920s. She credits it not so much to popularization of the automobile as to the crowded conditions of urban life that denied many young couples any sort of privacy during home visits. We can presume that marriageable daughters often tried (probably more or less successfully) to induce their parents to acquire presentable and modish living room furniture. Several retailers interviewed by *Photoplay Magazine* (1922, p.32) expressed such sentiments.

> If it were not for the younger generation, the furniture stores would go out of business. . . . The young folks come in with father or mother and tell what is the latest style . . . and usually the parents buy what the son or daughter suggest.

> I would say that seventy five percent of the furniture sold to the middle-aged people is because they want to have nice things for their daughters.

The late 19th and early 20th century was also a great period for the sale of musical instruments, phonographs, and music boxes (sometimes large console-type machines with repertoires of up to 75 tunes). Very likely, a major reason for purchasing this equipment was to ease the tension of those highly formal and stilted mating efforts (*The American Experience* 1989). Roehl (1989, p.27) reports that even considerably later, when the Victorian strictures had relaxed to the point where the young couple could be left together unchaperoned in the piano room with the doors closed, a popular song of the time warned the young lady to "keep your foot on the soft pedal.'' A *Photoplay Magazine* (1922, p.38) interview with a musical instrument merchant again demonstrates the influence of youth.

> From the high school age on, girls have quite a lot of influence in the purchase of pianos. About every high school girl wants music—a musical education seems almost a necessity to her in order to be able to entertain. Usually, the whole family comes to make the purchase, but the influence comes from the younger people, particularly the girls.

When automobile driving became popular in the 1920s and thereafter (Hart 1925), we can also guess that the glandular young swains wanted a car of their own or had thoughts about what their fathers should purchase, since the car offered ''an almost universal available means of escaping temporarily from the supervision of parents, chaperones, or from the influence of neighborhood opinion'' (Frederick 1931, p.100) and escape from ''traditional moral controls'' (Hart 1925, p.493). With respect to selling automobiles, Giles (1922, p.60) noted that ''a quick pressure on youth is often the best way to get the bigger, slower parent going.''

Safety bikes, those having two wheels of the same size, were popular by the 1890s. They were especially appealing to young people for the same mobility and freedom reasons that explain the later popularity of the automobile (Green 1986, p.225).

Of course many rural youths moved to the cities where they became part of the rooming and boarding house population (Peel 1986; Wolfe 1913). Young females who could not be supported in their rural homes often went to the mill town to work as machine operators and to be housed in company dormitories (Hall, et al. 1987).

Sons in working-class families often either established their own families or households or moved to live with relatives. The domicile change was designed to locate them nearer to work, but also to help them escape parental domination. Consequently, only the small minority who went on to college (see Table 2.2), plus the

TABLE 2.2

Population and education trends: 1880–1970

Year	Total U.S. population	Population 15–24 yr. olds	Percent 15–24 yr. olds	Percent 18–24 yr. olds in college	Percent of 17 yr. olds completing high school
1880	50,262	10,089	20.1	1.6	2.5
1890	63,056	12,744	20.2	1.8	3.5
1900	76,094	14,951	19.6	2.3	6.3
1910	92,407	18,212	19.7	2.9	8.6
1920	106,461	18,821	17.7	4.7	16.3
1930	123,077	22,487	16.9	7.2	28.8
1940	132,122	24,033	18.2	9.1	49.0
1950	151,684	22,260	14.7	14.2	57.4
1960	180,671	24,576	13.6	22.3	68.4
1970	204,879	36,496	17.8	32.1	75.6

Population figures in thousands.

Source: *Historical Statistics of the United States, Colonial Times to 1970: Bicentennial Issues, Part 1* (1975), Washington, D.C.: Government Printing Office.

young men who remained on the family farm and the young women who stayed on "to help mother," were likely to be able to influence family consumption.

A common theme expressed by a number of commentators was youth's influence on older age segments.

> If you sell the young people of the land, you will at the same moment, sell the older people (Larned 1921, p.154).

> The cigarette which was popularized entirely by youth has easily won its more mature following as a sequel (Giles 1922, p.60).

But perhaps of just as great importance was the influence of college students. Bailey (1988, p.145–6) observed:

. . . college culture exerted influence and carried a symbolic weight much greater than the actual number and role that college students would justify. Even in the early twentieth century, the conventions and customs of college students were presented to the nation in minute detail by popular magazines and found a fascinated public. College customs probably influenced the culture-at-large as much as vice versa.

A number of fashion trends originated among college youth including soft-collared shirts, low-heeled winter Oxfords, and non-gartered socks. College students set trends for younger as well as older individuals.

If you sell the college man, you sell the many younger lads who are taking the college hero as their ideal (p.1072) . . . . The country follows the lead of the college student in matters of dress (Russell 1926, p.1105).

The rise in the second half of the 19th century of a large commercial beauty culture (Banner 1983) has implications for the effect of youth (or at least of youthfulness) on other age segments. This industry included many service establishments such as hairdressers, massage parlors, pedicure establishments, as well as manufacturers of cosmetics and feminine wearing apparel. The prevailing idea of beauty changed from time to time; the ideal was voluptuous before the turn of the century, tall and aristocratic as epitomized by the Gibson Girl between 1900 and 1910, and reckless and independent as revealed by the boyish Flapper Girl during the 1920s (Richards 1951). But always the emphasis for many customers has been on youthfulness, or at least in appearing younger than they actually were. Removing signs of aging was a prime objective. "In any event, the commercial beauty culture played a powerful role in standardizing the connection between beauty and youth" (Banner 1983, p.225).

The link between youth and beauty was recognized and taken advantage of by advertisers. Youth appeal ads that stressed beauty or healthfulness (see *Advertising Age* 1988, p.40, for a 1920 example) were discussed by marketing commentators (Carmical 1928; Emmett 1926), and this type of campaign, like the 1960s' Pepsi campaign, may not have been entirely or even mainly youth segmentation driven. Product positioning along a youthful dimension may be successful because of:

> The tendency for people of all ages to dress in the manner of youth, to act as young people do, to think as young people do, and to make believe, so far as may be possible, that they are young people (Nystrom 1928, p.74).

The College Market

Frederick Russell (1926), a professor of business at the University of Illinois, provided several reasons for the increasing importance of the college youth segment.

1. Between 1890 and 1924, the number of college students in the United States grew from 121,942 to 664,266, an increase of 445 percent, representing a growth rate about six times that of the population.

2. Colleges were no longer isolated repositories that cloistered the young from the remainder of society. Better roads played a major role. Conventions were regularly scheduled on campuses, and football and other sporting events attracted thousands of people.

3. High school students were increasingly aware of colleges and campus life. They participated in regional sporting events (e.g., track meets, basketball tournaments), and they visited colleges on educational field trips. College students, therefore, affected their purchasing decisions.

4. College graduates remain collegiate in dress long after graduation. Hence, the college student is sold to for more than four years.

5. The increasingly practical nature of college curricula (i.e., the inclusion of courses in business, engineering, and agriculture), especially among land grant institutions, meant that graduates were able to obtain a high standard of living much quicker than those who studied under the system that stressed the study of classics.

6. College students were developing unique tastes for clothing which were ''ahead of the average community in matter of style'' (p.1072). A seller gaining acceptance of dress among college students would, after a time, find the remainder of the population more receptive.

7. Not only was the growth rate of female participation increasing at a rate faster than that of males, the increasing number of co-ed institutions meant that both sexes were spending more on health and beauty aids.

8. Parental influence over college student purchasing behavior was not only declining, but children were beginning to affect parental choices of automobiles and clothing.

Many of Russell's observations overlap with those already made in this chapter. But he does capture the essence of why the college market was *increasingly* important. And, by implication, it was already an important market.

Another question concerns how applicable his points are to urban educational institutions and particularly to those that catered to much more of a working class and commuter population. Probably the non-socially elite city schools contained many individuals who, to the best of their financial ability and to the extent that circumstances permitted, tried to ape the stereotype of college life. They also would have been in contact with many noncollegiate peers and thus would have been a conduit for consumption incluence from the academic to the nonacademic environment. Russell concluded his discussion by saying (p.1005):

> No one can afford to overlook a market which is increasing so rapidly in size and importance as the American college market.

CHAPTER THREE

Early Promotional Practices

As we saw in Chapter 2, it is clear that writers of the 1880–1940 period recognized the importance of selling to youth. We have not provided evidence yet to support the belief that segmentation or positioning occurred. To accomplish that, this chapter describes promotional practices and discusses the 'advertising literature of the period. In Exhibit 3.1 on the following page a summary of the literature on all the elements of the marketing mix—promotion, price, distribution, product—is presented.

Conceptually, the distinction between segmentation, as defined here, and product differentiation is clear (Smith 1956). In practice, it often becomes fuzzy. Much youth marketing in particular seems to consist primarily in saying that the product is youthful

EXHIBIT 3.1
Literature summary: How youth was sold to (1880–1940)

Topic	Selected citations (alphabetical order)

Promotion

Advertising to youth	*Bulletin NRDGA* 1938a; Larned 1927; Nichols 1919; North 1929; *Photoplay Magazine* 1922; *Printers' Ink* 1904a, 1905a, 1915a, 1919, 1920d, 1922, 1924, 1936; Russell 1926; *Sales Management* 1936; Travis 1926; Vance 1896
Educational material	McDonough 1938; Palmer and Schlink 1934; *Printers' Ink* 1915b, 1915c, 1916, 1926, 1931; *Printers' Ink Monthly* 1938
Contests/ games	Dickinson 1932; Howe 1931; *Printers' Ink* 1905c, 1915a, 1924, 1935, 1937
Special promotions	Ellison 1934; *Printers' Ink* 1915a, 1935; Vance 1896
Direct mail	Dumont 1929; *Printers' Ink* 1935
Price	*Bulletin NRDGA* 1938b; Cobb 1921; Clark 1924; *Printers' Ink* 1896; Vance 1896
Distribution	Ballard 1919; *Bulletin NRDGA* 1939; Burns 1926; Dumont 1929; Fallows 1901; Jacobson 1928; *Journal of Retailing* 1928; Lyons 1933; McNair and Gragg 1930; Nemetz 1939; Palmer and Schlink 1934; *Printers' Ink* 1915c, 1935; *Printers' Ink Monthly* 1938; Schacter 1930; Sinsheimer 1926; Yocum 1934

Product

Special trades	*Bulletin NRDGA* 1938b, 1938c; Donovan 1938; Hanson 1940; Lyons 1933; Vincent 1925
Product design	DeCamp 1929; Donnell 1940; Frederick 1929; Lewis 1933; *Photoplay Magazine* 1922; *Printers' Ink* 1904a; Vance 1896

rather than imbuing it with special physical attributes or offering it at special places or prices. Promotion, for example, seems to be the primary component of the Pepsi Generation segmentation strategy which we have designated as "positioning." In other instances, such as this extreme example, college insignia T-shirts, product design and place of distribution are crucial. But given the importance of promotion in youth segmentation, we will describe a number of instances in which promotion was either the major key or sole element in such segmentation.

ADVERTISING

Advertising agencies published newspaper and magazine directories that presented publication listings by "class" as early as 1882. (Edwin Alden & Bro's 1882; N.W. Ayer & Son's 1882). These classes were grouped according to topical material or reader similarity and included religious, college, agricultural, juvenile, and scientific classes. Each class was further broken down by state and each publication listing included a circulation estimate and frequency of publication information. A list of printed media most likely to reach a desired "segment" was readily available well before the turn of the century.

The Collegiate Special Advertising Agency, Inc. (CSAA), established in 1914, specialized in obtaining national (i.e., nonlocal) advertising for campus publications. One of CSAA house ads taken from a 1927 issue of *Printer's Ink* is shown in Exhibit 3.2. The ad publicizes a CSAA promotional directory, the *Collegiate Salesman* (a listing of college publications). The existence of CSAA provides evidence that the industry segmented the market on the type of customer, and that one of those customer types was youth. In 1928, CSAA issued *The Local Ad Handbook* as a goodwill device to help train campus newspaper and magazine staffs in the art of securing *local* advertising. Although modestly produced (by mimeograph

EXHIBIT 3.2
Advertising agency ad

Student Stores Are Growing!

The aggregate business done by the four Cooperative Stores at Harvard, Cornell, Princeton and Yale was over two million dollars last year—or more than double what it was eight years ago.

Have you ever considered what it means to sell in a market which is expanding so quickly? Business increases automatically. The number of students at college has doubled in ten years.

We can show you how to sell your product thru supply stores and other stores that get college trade. We have been doing it for fourteen years.

Ask us anything you want to know about the school or college market.

The revised "Collegiate Salesman" containing complete lists of collegiate publications will be sent upon request.

Established 1013

Collegiate Special Advertising Agency, Inc.

503 Fifth Ave., New York
612 No. Michigan Ave., Chicago

From: *Printers' Ink* (1927), 140 (July 14), 168.

or some other near-printing process), the 55-page, 8-½" × 11" manual provided helpful advice on space selling and client development. Exhibit 3.3 presents a list of local establishments that campus publications should seek as advertisers (as suggested by The *Local Ad Handbook*).

In spite of the availability of collegiate and noncollegiate publication listings and the existence of the CSAA, a review of several scattered issues of college newspapers retained in the Warshaw files (e.g., *Cornell Daily Sun* 1902; *Yale Courant* 1874; *Yale News* 1890) revealed that the majority of ads were local in nature and that most did not specifically mention collegiate or noncollegiate youth. An analysis of several scattered 1920 issues of *College Humor* revealed that most of the ads did not specifically mention youth. This fact, however, is somewhat misleading. Large half- or full-page ads appeared for Schlitz beer in the October 1902 issue of *Cornell Humor*, for Remington typewriters in the *Cornell Daily Sun*, and for Listerine, Life Savers, and Pepsodent, among others, in *College Humor* during the 1920s. While the *College Humor* ads failed to mention youth, they depicted attractive youth in product-usage scenarios.

College Humor provides a striking example of youth segmentation. It was directed primarily to youth, it advertised itself as a suitable youth-reaching medium (e.g., *Sales Management* 1929, April 13, p. 81), it offered to conduct research of a product's potential within the college market, and it made available free of charge a 72-page booklet entitled *An Approach to the College Market* (*College Humor* 1928). The booklet contained the results of a series of readership studies, one of which reported that 22 percent of 16,696 college students regularly read *College Humor*. Apparently, the booklet was primarily a promotional tool used by the magazine to attract advertisers.

Many college newspaper ads mentioning youth were placed by local service establishments such as barber and food shops, dance halls, and laundry establishments. By 1915, specially designed half- and full-page ads for Fatima cigarettes were appearing in 30 college newspapers, along with ads for Pall Mall, Omars, and

EXHIBIT 3.3
Local ad prospects for campus publications

1. *School Supplies.* The first and most obvious classification is that of school supplies. This includes school books, stationery, typewriters, etc. Possibly you have a store right in your school, otherwise you will find this type of store located very near the college.

2. *Things to Wear.* Haberdashers, clothiers, custom tailors, hatters, shoe stores, etc.

3. *Drug Stores.* A college drug store very often carries many other items besides those which are found in the average drug store and it is always a good prospect for advertising. They have many things to feature including their soda fountain, confectionery, smokers' articles, toilet articles, medicines, etc. Very often you will find a separate shop for some of these articles—such as tobacco or confectionery or candy or nuts.

4. *Sporting Goods and Athletics.* This is found in either a special or individual store or in your general supply store or in a drug store or hardware store.

5. *Women's Specialty Shops and Department Stores.* Many of the other classifications listed in this section will be found as a department in a large department store. Though as a rule men don't like to trade in department stores, women do.

6. *Amusements.* Movies, theaters, restaurants, road houses, cabarets, dance halls, amusement parks, lecture and concert halls, bowling alleys, pool parlors, aeroplane rides, skating rinks, tennis courts, golf courses. Restaurants would also come under another classification for their utility value together with cafeterias, automats, soda fountains.

7. *Travel.* Hotels, railroads, natural wonders, travel and tour agencies, trolley and bus lines, autos for hire, taxi service, aeroplane service.

8. *Miscellaneous Domestic Services.* Cleaners and dyers, tailors, laundries, fuel (coal and ice dealers).

9. *Music.* Music stores, radio stores, instrument stores.

10. *Orchestras for Hire.*

EXHIBIT 3.3

Local ad prospects for campus publications (*continued*)

11. *Local and Sectional Daily and Weekly Newspapers.*

12. *Furniture.*

13. *Luggage and Trunks and Umbrellas.*

14. *Printers.*

15. *Grocers.*

16. *Undertakers.*

17. *Schools.* Shorthand, music, dancing, business colleges, driving schools, flying schools, graduate schools, professional colleges, personal tutoring. You may find that your own school is a good prospect for advertising. Schools advertise in their own college paper for prestige and to keep students in the school. Schools often advertise special courses and graduate and professional courses in their school paper.

18. *Bakeries.*

19. *Public stenographers.*

20. *Political Advertising.* At election time political organizations are willing to spend money to promote their interests. Watch your credit risk in this kind of business.

21. *Medical Service.* Doctors, dentists, opticians, chiropractors, osteopaths.

22. *Finance.* Banks, pawn shops, loan brokers, building and loan companies, insurance, fire, burglary, life.

23. *Barber Shops, Hairdressers and Beauty Parlors.*

24. *Repair Services.* Furniture, typewriters, automobiles, fountain pens, shoes, watches.

25. *Shirt Hospitals.*

26. *Churches.*

27. *Plumbers.*

28. *Decorators and Painters.* Picture framing, art supplies, gift novelties.

29. *Public Utilities.* Power, light and heat, telephone service.

30. *Traction Companies.*

EXHIBIT 3.3
Local ad prospects for campus publications (*continued*)

31. *Florists.*

32. *Jewelers and Fraternity Jewelers.*

33. *Hardware.*

34. *Photographers and Camera Supplies.*

35. *Express Companies.*

36. *Automobile Field.* New and second hand automobile dealers, garages, gas stations, automobile accessories.

37. *Tuxedo Rental and Costume Rental.*

38. *Camps.*

39. *Teachers' Agencies.*

40. *Employment Agencies.*

41. *Student Agents.* There are always some students who will work their way through school by selling various objects. Very often they will advertise in a small way in your publication.

42. *School Organizations.* Some papers make it a practice to give free advertising space to official school athletic events and official social events. If handled properly, these should be a source of revenue. Any activity in your school which operates on a business basis should be made to pay its own way. If there is another publication at your school, possibly you can exchange advertising space to mutual advantage.

43. *Philatelists.* You would be surprised how many students would be interested in stamp collecting as a hobby.

Source: Collegiate Special Advertising Agency, Inc. (1928), *The Local Ad Handbook*, New York: Collegiate Special Advertising Agency, Inc., p.5–8.

Deities (*Printers' Ink* 1915a). *Printers' Ink* (1922, p. 8) noted that "a single piece of copy for all prospects has gone the way of many other things which have been discarded in the business of advertising." Distinct ads created by Williams' Shaving Cream for college publications sought to "speak a language understood by college students" (*Printers' Ink* 1922, p. 8). The Illinois Central System placed special ads in college newspapers located on or near their rail lines (*Printers' Ink* 1936) for the purpose of increasing rail service consumption. Companies like General Electric (*Printers' Ink* 1920d) and Westinghouse (Travis 1926) conducted goodwill and recruitment campaigns in college newspapers across the nation.

Ads specifically mentioning collegiate or noncollegiate youth were found in various 1920 issues of *College Humor* for Dodge autos, Philco radios, Kodak cameras, Goodyear athletic shoes and Bradley knitwear (college insignia sweaters). Especially common were ads promoting self-taught music lessons appealing to a youth's desire to be popular. This is consistent with the finding reported by *Photoplay Magazine* (1922) that 48 percent of wind instrument purchases were made by youth between the ages of 18 and 30 (Refer to Table 2.1).

A Dodge ad in *College Humor* (1933, November, p. 118) said, "Youth votes this new Dodge a winner at $595." Although Tedlow (1990, p. 180) noted "neither life-style nor demographics appeared to be uppermost in GM's definition of consumer segments," the Dodge ad indicates that part of Dodge's advertising strategy described the "low price" segment at least in terms of age and youth. Chevrolet also ran "bull's eye copy" ads. Townsend (1924, p. 144) described one Chevrolet ad as "a specifically addressed advertising message to young women stenographers."

Many youth marketing ads were placed in newspapers. In one, Wanamaker extolled a hat designed for young men (*Printers' Ink* 1904a). *Printers' Ink* (1905a) praised another that promoted gas stoves to young women. The copy, accompanied by a drawing of a young woman, explained that a gas stove would save time and help create superior culinary delights. The gas stove ad and the *Photoplay Magazine* (1922) study are exceptions to the observation that appliance/home furnishing makers did not exploit the youth market.

Sporting goods manufacturers mounted a national newspaper advertising campaign with the goal of having Congress repeal a 10 percent excise tax on the sale of their products (Nichols 1919). In this effort, whether with the aim of impressing youth themselves or of striking a sympathetic chord among older generations, we cannot say, but the manufacturers did point out that 70 percent of their output was purchased by or for those under the age of 18.

The National Retail Dry Goods Association—the department store trade association (NRDGA) later known as the National Retail Merchants Association and now National Retail Federation—urged its members in 1938 to participate actively in Father's Day promotions. It told them that this occasion, which department stores had generally neglected during the preceding 25 years, provided an opportunity to make profitable sales to a market that consisted primarily of wives, daughters, and, to a lesser extent, sons. It suggested establishing gift centers within the store or place at which merchandise priced within the younger customer's budget would be located, and noted that young men at college could be reached through the ubiquitous college newspapers (*Bulletin NRDGA* 1938a).

Many advertisers who hoped to sell to older as well as to younger consumers stressed youthfulness in their message. This was particularly true of firms that dealt in appearance-related products such as apparel and health and beauty aids. Cluett-Peabody Co. was responsible for one of the best known pre-World War I advertising campaigns—a long-running campaign based upon the incredibly handsome, if somewhat priggish looking, Arrow Collar Man. That advertising campaign (until displaced by the rising popularity of the collar attached shirt, itself a youth-caused innovation) led innumerable men into using stiff, highly uncomfortable starched collars.

A somewhat later (1930s) promotion aimed at the other gender was Cheeseburough-Pond's, "She's Lovely, She's Engaged, She Uses Ponds." These advertisements featured attractive young society women who were engaged to be married (and who apparently, in the Depression years of the 1930s, were glad to add a Pond's fee to their dowries).

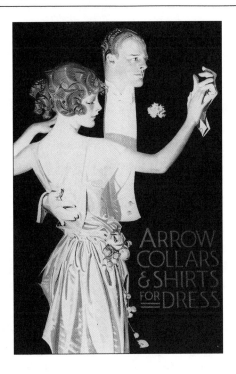

Another major youth-based campaign was created around the "Jantzen Girl" logo—a gracefully arched, youthful female diver. By 1928, it was the seventh best-known trademark in the United States. One of the campaign's objectives was to convince the American public to "embrace swimming as a major leisure activity" (Lencek and Bosker 1988, p. 48). In fact, Wallis (1959) credits Jantzen with introducing the term swimsuit to the American public. The "quest for the suntan, symbolizing the healthy glow of youth," along with the freedom of dress, popularized swimming for all age groups throughout the century (Braden and Endelman 1990, p. 66). The molding of a favorable public opinion toward swimming and the use of youthful models allowed Jantzen to market form revealing swimsuits that were scandalous by the standards of the day.

The Jordan Motor Car Company's "Somewhere West of Laramie" ad promoting the Playboy automobile, appearing in the mid 1920s, was listed by Watkins (1949) as one of the 100 greatest ads. The ad depicts a female driving a Playboy racing against a cowboy on horseback and says:

Somewhere west of Laramie there's a bronco-busting, steer-roping girl who knows what I'm talking about. She can tell what a sassy pony, that's a cross between greased lightening and the place where it hits, can do with eleven hundred pounds of steel and action when he's going high, wide and handsome (p. 51).

According to Watkins, the ad broke all the rules, yet "sales struck lighting" (p. 51) and the public read the ad, recited it, and stored it away. Whether or not the ad was a willful attempt at psychographic segmentation with a youthful angle we cannot say, but it certainly resulted in creating an image for the Playboy automobile that was western and youthful.

Hallmark Cards designed its teenage-targeted "Betty Betz" line during the mid-1940s. Hallmark promoted the line as "greeting cards that speak the Coke Set lingo" and as "groovy new greeting cards designed just for you [teenagers]" (Rich 1991). The ad from which the quotations were taken was run in 96 cities with total newspaper circulation approaching 30 million.

The Hallmark Cards campaign tapped into the youth slang and culture of the period. Usage of groovy as meaning "in a state of mind or conducive to playing music" is documented to 1935 among swing-jive musicians and afficionados (Wentworth and Flexner 1967, p. 232), and its link to the more modern (post-1950s) meaning of cool is quite clear.

In spite of the fact that Tedlow (1990) saw Coca-Cola as a Phase II supplier before and well after 1940, he also saw the soft drink supplier quite successfully creating a youthful image for its product. With respect to a series of 1901–1919 calendar and poster promotions featuring youthful models, Tedlow (p. 48) said:

"Pretty Girls," . . . presented an ideal of femininity. Young women aspired to be like the girls in the advertisements; young men aspired to date them. And these girls drank Coca-Cola. By drinking Coca-Cola—for only a nickel a bottle—Americans could associate themselves, in their own minds at least, with the world in which winsome girls such as these seemed to dwell.

Coca-Cola also featured youthful models in their 1920s campaign to increase winter season consumption (Watkins 1949, p. 139). Slang associated with Coca-Cola found its way into advertising and popular usage. The Hallmark Cards ad mentioned the Coke Set, a fictional, groovy youth subculture that was an early counterpart to the 1960s Pepsi generation. Coke Date referred to a non-alcoholic adolescent date. And Coke Frame, clearly a chauvinistic term, arose during the 1930s and referred to "a shapely girl or woman whose figure resembled the shape of a Coca-Cola bottle" (Wentworth and Flexner 1967, p. 114).

Carmical (1928) reported that the vast majority (just how vast we are uncertain) of 167 ads in an issue of a popular magazine revealed "the ever increasing trend toward dramatization and appealing to youth" (p. 674). Of course, a cross-sectional study cannot reveal a longitudinal trend. In any event, he observed that advertisers were eager to associate their products with youth: rubber heels "conserve energy and keep us young;" scalp preparations "keep one from looking old and neglected;" and a shoe supplier depicted a young girl as follows: "down the boardwalk she came—as graceful as a cresting wave—as light as breeze-blown foam" (p. 674).

Richard Pollay (1985) conducted a content analysis of a scientifically selected sample of 2,000 advertisements drawn from popular U.S. magazines from 1900 through 1979. His sample included 250 items from each decade. Of the 1920s, he writes (p. 111):

> Perhaps because of the nature of these products [health and beauty aids and packaged foods that dominated the advertising of the period], but also consistent with the flapper era's image as youth-oriented, the advertising appeals that predominate are those of sexiness (26%) and youthfulness, peaking in this decade at 11% of all ads.

Pollay's study provides empirical evidence that youthful images were widespread in advertising during the 1920s, and that youthfulness in advertising has yet to regain its 1920s stature.

''The image of the 'flapper ad' of the 'bright young things' is part of the myth rather than the reality of the 1920s'' according to Maltby (1989, p. 76). He comments on a drawing of a seated, short-skirted, cross-legged young woman exposing a startling expanse of hosiery, thigh, and garter to the apparent delight of a nearby observant male.

> Only a few rich young women had the freedom, leisure and daring to engage in affairs outside marriage. Skirts never rose above the knee and the glimpse of suspender [British garter] would have been an embarrassment for a real life young woman, although such awkwardness did actually occur (Maltby 1989, p. 76).

However, on page 13, he also says:

> In the 1920s, the ''flapper'' as a beautiful woman was an ubiquitous advertising image. She was, as social historian Stuart Ewen put it: ''pure consumer, dancing through the world of material goods. She was young, marked by energy, not judgment. Her clothes, her vehicle, her entire milieu was mass-produced—and she liked it.''

The validity of Maltby's conclusions about the relative rarity of flappers might be considered a matter of definition. How did a young woman qualify? What was sufficient—wearing bobbed hair, dancing the Charleston, engaging in extramarital sex? Some moralists probably considered all three activities equally wicked, interchangeable, and interrelated. More meaningfully, the comment can be generalized. As we point out elsewhere, the advertiser's pictures of youth, particularly when presented to nonyouth, is almost always oversimplified, exhilarated, sociable, energetic, and carefree beyond all reality. Even the fear ads (''Often a Bridesmaid, Never a Bride'') that did suggest that all was not sweetness and light in Youthsville, always offered a quick and easy solution. The fictitious sophistication of the flapper in the 1920s ad probably was no more simplistic than the unadulterated wholesome good humor of the teen-age beach parties in more contemporary Pepsi ads.

EDUCATIONAL CAMPAIGNS

Companies and other organizations conducted a wide variety of promotional efforts designed to reach youth in the classroom. Since maintaining student lists was prohibitively expensive, the most critical element in the distribution and acceptance of educational material was the professor (or teacher) who was viewed as "the middleman between us [the company] and the student" (*Printers' Ink* 1915c, p. 11). The ultimate goals of such efforts were wide ranging. Increased brand (*Printers' Ink* 1931; Palmer and Schlink 1934) and corporate awareness (Bryant 1990) were two such goals for current and future consumption in both consumer and industrial contexts (*Printers' Ink* 1916: *Printers' Ink Monthly* 1938). C. Hirschberg of Ingersoll–Rand said that "we look upon college men in the same light as we look upon the office-boy of a prospective customer. We cultivate him and make a friend of him because some day he might be president'' (*Printers' Ink* 1915c, p. 11). Ingersoll–Rand apparently was willing to court potential future buyers wherever they could be located.

The work of Burr Blackburn, a social worker who organized the consumer education department of Household Finance Corporation (now Household International) in 1930, provides an example of a public service educational campaign. In this case, the goal was to increase consumer knowledge of personal and family money management, as well as that of building goodwill for the corporation. The department's first thrust was the publication of a series of *Better Buymanship* and *Money Management* booklets. Of the six million booklets distributed between 1930 and 1941, the greatest proportion went to schools and colleges in response to advertising in educational periodicals. About 40 percent were sent to HFC offices and the remainder were distributed to YMCAs and various social agencies. During the same period, over a million individuals viewed at least one of the department's five motion picture or five sound slide shows. In 1941, Blackburn said:

> Over a period of ten years we have been able to build confidence and understanding in our program, and that confidence is based largely on the fact that we have so carefully refrained from using the program for direct advertising of any kind, or any kind of public relations program. We have strictly done a consumer educational job and it is so exceptional and unusual for a commercial agency to take that attitude that doors have been opened to us that have not been opened to any other type of commercial material (Bryant 1990, p. 4).

Household International has continued its consumer education activity through what it now calls its Money Management Institute (Bryant 1990).

Another goal of educational campaigns was to influence the parents of school-aged youth, although in some cases several age segments were reached. RCA Victor spent $100,000 (the equivalent of millions of dollars today) in educational periodicals and direct mail to convince educators of the value of phonographic music history lessons (*Printers' Ink* 1915b). RCA was "able to trace directly a growth in general sales following the placing of Victor machines in the schools of a city" (*Printers' Ink* 1915b, p. 18).

The manufacturers who benefitted the most from supplying educational material probably were the ones who trained future operators of their equipment. In some instances they sponsored schools of their own. Shortly after the Gregg shorthand system was introduced in the United States in 1893 as a rival to the prevailing Pitman systems, the Gregg publisher moved to cultivate teachers of shorthand. It established the *Business Education World*, a professional journal for such teachers, and it provided a stable of speakers for local, state, and national shorthand teachers. Gregg also established its own school in Chicago, which not only provided instruction to future stenographers, but also trained many teachers and strongly influenced vocational office education (Forkner and DeYoung 1976).

Typewriter sales lagged until the 1880s, in part because the low wages paid for typing work failed to attract young men, then considered the only appropriate candidates for entry-level office jobs. In 1881, a New York City YWCA introduced a typing course for young ladies, all of whom found immediate employment. The YWCA courses proliferated and the market-oriented management of the Remington Typewriter Company quickly arranged for the creation of an extensive network of Remington Typing Schools both in the United States and abroad (Bliven 1954, p. 31-9). The schools, of course, were not limited to youth but apparently appealed most to young ladies. The result was not only the development of a market for Remington machines, but also a major change in the gender composition of office personnel.

Typewriter and office business machine manufacturers were very anxious to obtain school (particularly high school) adoption of their particular equipment. They sold machines for classroom instruction at lower prices than the institutions were charged for identical equipment to be used for administrative purposes. This led to a certain amount of duplicity in the way in which some schools ordered their own supplies. The manufacturers also assiduously cultivated high school and collegiate teachers of business education. They maintained hospitality suites at teachers' conferences, supplied teaching aids, educational monographs, and classroom exercises and also were willing to provide lecturers for conferences and seminars. Interestingly, the manufacturers were either ambivalent or negative toward attempts to popularize elementary school typing and business machine instruction. They feared that such instruction would tend to reduce public respect for typing skills. The companies maintained stables of speed typists who participated in high prize ($10,000) national speed-typing contests that generated exercises for classroom purposes. They also supported other contestants (Lloyd 1990).

In 1926, Deere & Company found that promotional posters were being used by agricultural and mechanical educators. This spawned a new series of educational posters, and, by 1945, over a half million had been distributed. In 1927, Deere published a mechanics textbook that, according to H. Railsback (1945), Deere's director of advertising, "covers practically all the machines in the John Deere line." By 1945, the book was in its 18th edition and over two million copies had been distributed. In 1936, the company also began distributing student project record books free of charge. Railsback also commented on how such materials not only influenced future purchasers, but led the young men to influence their fathers.

Beginning in the 1920s, piano manufacturers Steinway and Sons and, especially, the Baldwin Company assiduously cultivated music teachers. They lent instruments to the teachers and paid them commissions for successful sales leads. Baldwin encouraged high school and college music classes, and the industry's trade association worked for increased music education in the public schools (Roehl 1989, p. 171).

In 1937, five department stores contributed $2,500, and a group of manufacturers—of fabrics, sewing materials, and patterns—contributed $5,000 to establish the San Francisco branch of the Sewing Institute. Its main function was to persuade the city's Board of Education to increase emphasis and support for sewing classes and to encourage those classes to deal with a wider range of styles, garments, and (presumably more expensive) fabrics. The results were reported as gratifying, but the manufacturers felt that stores in any other city that wanted a similar program should underwrite the full cost (McDonough 1938). We wonder if the promotion would not be suboptimal for stores that also sold ready-made garments, but their fabric department managers would not see it that way.

Marketers tried not only to get material favorable to their interests included in the curricula; on at least one occasion, they worked quite vigorously to have material they considered unfavorable excluded. In 1939–40, several leaders of the advertising and media industries mounted a strenuous campaign against what they claimed were subversive and/or anti-advertising college and secondary school texts. Much of the debate focused on statements about the cost of advertising. Strong criticism was directed against *An Introduction to Problems of American Culture* (1931), a high school text written by Professor Harold Rugg of Columbia University, even though that book contained relatively supporting conclusions about the need for sales promotion in a complex economy (Sorenson 1941, p. 159–65).

CONTESTS/GAMES

Games and contests, while more prevalent in marketing to children, were used to reach collegiate and noncollegiate youth. In some instances, games were directed to children, adolescents, and youth simultaneously. The Hood Rubber Co., a maker of canvas running shoes used by 5 to 19 year olds, sponsored a "cryptogram" contest that was promoted in juvenile magazines. Dealers purchased 200,000 ad reprints, 350,000 copies of a "secret writing book" and one million handbills. In the end, over 160,000 game entries were received, and a number of new, tough-to-crack dealers were added to the company's distribution system (Dickinson 1932; Howe 1931).

In other instances, games were targeted to collegiate youth. The Vortex Cup Company, a maker and distributor of office sup-

plies, created and distributed a game to college fraternities (*Printers'
Ink* 1935). The objective was to raise awareness of the company's
brand for future industrial purposes.

Fatima, a cigarette supplier, asked collegiate youth to create college newspaper ads. The winner received a monetary prize and the
winning submission was run in college newspapers (*Printers' Ink*
1915a). Camel Pen Company offered prizes up to $150 to the student
who wrote the best marketing plan for the company's new products
(*Printers' Ink* 1937). And the Union Trust Company, Detroit, annually awarded five $1,000 university scholarships to young men and
women who wrote bank-related essays (*Printers' Ink* 1924).

Society Brands Clothes, who promoted themselves as a maker
of collegiate styled men's suits, sponsored a contest in which ten
of 15,00 entrants were winners because of "their embodiment of
the correct thing in college style" (*College Humor* 1927, October, p.
6). The winners appeared in "Drop Kick," a Hollywood movie,
and with the contest sponsor, were supposed to guarantee the real-
ism of the college styles depicted in the film.

SPECIAL PROMOTIONS

The distribution of free or discounted tobacco samples to college
and university students (*Printers' Ink* 1915a; Vance 1896) is an
example of a special promotion. In 1928, Deere & Company began
giving miniature engraved plows to Future Farmers of America
chapters for ceremonial purposes (Railsback 1945). Brunswick, a
maker of billiard tables, concluded that declining sales to pool halls
were the result of young men not taking up the activity, in spite
of increases in the amount of money spent on recreational activities
(Ellison 1934). Free billiard lessons were test marketed in three
cities with the following results: (1) 43 percent of those who took
lessons had never played before; and (2) mean daily revenue of
participating pool halls increased from $54 to $77 (a substantial

sum in those days). A comprehensive marketing plan was developed and implemented across the nation.

The Jantzen campaign mentioned earlier, which involved much more than just selling a product, attempted to favorably adjust society's morals and opinions to better suit corporate needs. This is similar to one of Edward Bernays' 1929 publicity efforts. Debutantes were a particularly useful subset of the youth market for promotional purposes. Bernays, public relations counsel for the American Tobacco Company, persuaded ten debutantes to smoke while strolling on Fifth Avenue in the traditional Easter Sunday fashion parade. They were told that they were striking a blow for women's liberation, but American Tobacco was primarily interested in breaking the taboo against female consumption of tobacco in public places. Bernays (1965), not exactly a shrinking violet, claims that this single promotional activity obtained national publicity, induced widespread discussion, and caused multiple breaches in the taboo (much like Jantzen did with the wearing of skimpy swimsuits).

DIRECT MAIL

Companies often mailed cards directly to college fraternities informing them of the nearest local dealer for their product. Spangles, a dance hall product (Dumont 1929), and Vortex Cups (*Printers' Ink* 1935), provide examples.

One aspect of direct mail that yields evidence of youth marketing is mail order catalogues. A number of catalogues were analyzed: R.H. Macy (1884), Towne and Country (1908), Stern Brothers (1898), V. Bedell (1915), B. Altman (1882; 1913; 1924; 1925), as well as fashion brochures printed by menswear manufacturers/wholesalers such as Hart Schaffner & Marx (1903; 1915), B.R. Baker (1922), and Henry Estes Outfitter (1905).

In the earlier catalogues, little attempt appears to have been made to separate youth from children and adults. The addition of *misses* styles began to appear (Towne and Country 1908) very early in the century, but while the lines were differentiated, the departments or sections were not.

Misses-sized garments in mail order catalogues were frequently priced lower than women's sizes, and price-sensitive adults who were slender enough were encouraged to order larger misses sizes.

By the 1920s (and much earlier in some instances), college styles began to be featured in promotional brochures that menswear firms supplied to dealers for their customers. A 1903 "Style Book" published by Hart Schaffner & Marx contained numerous drawings of the correct thing in style and stated:

> This season you will find four distinct styles in sack suits: the regular single-breasted and double-breasted sacks, and the famous "Varsity," which is made in double-breasted as well as single-breasted style. You probably know something of the H S & M "Varsity"; our name for a sack suit especially for *young* men—college fellows, the younger business men, and the older ones whose tastes in clothing matters keep young. The "Varsity" coat is somewhat shorter than the regular sack, and the general lines are slightly different, giving it a jaunty, "young men's" look . . . We have taken the question of clothes for these young fellows seriously; our "Varsity" styles exactly fills this *middle ground*. [emphasis supplied]

Other Hart Schaffner & Marx style books published during the 1910s continued to emphasize "Varsity" and young men styles. Their 1915 "Style Book for Men and Young Men" focused more on Varsity and young men's clothing than on more established clothing lines. A 1925 B. Altman catalogue said, "Chic is the word when shopping for the younger set," and a 1922 B.R. Baker brochure featured a special collegiate page and said, "College men, they certainly know 'style'."

In short, by the 1920s, mail order and other apparel retailers were specifically designating certain garments as appropriate for youth. To enhance the appeal of the styles, retailers associated them with collegiate youth.

CHAPTER FOUR

Price and Distribution

In spite of their limited financial resources, it was recognized that youth were less price sensitive than older individuals (Cobb 1921). Vance (1896, p.21) noted that "college students are rather liberal, and do not hesitate to pay good prices for good things." Pecuniary considerations led some firms to offer price discounts to youth or students, especially in relation to entertainment and leisure. Clark (1924, reported by Backman, 1953, p.280) noted that many theaters offered educational discounts on tickets. Play-going was, of course, a more pervasive form of entertainment than today. However, such tickets were normally available only for "morally uplifting" productions that were unable to attract full houses of full-price customers away from more popular musical comedies.

One summer resort offered "special rates to young men" (*Printers' Ink* 1896). This was good business practice because the resort that "welcomes young men is sure to have the opportunity of likewise welcoming young women [along with chaperones]— droves of them" (p.8), hopefully at full price. The tactic seems reasonable. A major function of resorts was to provide opportunities for socializing, flirting, and courtship under somewhat more relaxed social strictures than applied in urban life (Braden and Endelman 1990, 52–4). The technique is also transferable across age segments. Some modern cruise line operators now offer discounted or free travel to personable, unattached older men who will pay attention to female passengers desiring companionship. Braden and Endelman (1990) also note that women, children, and unmarried young adults tended to stay for weeks or the entire summer, while fathers remained in the city or visited on weekends, and that "by the end of the nineteenth century, enterprising businessmen were catering to and exploiting resort-goers" (p.53).

One of the authors recalls using a reduced rate student multiple-ride ticket on the Long Island Railroad (a Pennsylvania Railroad subsidiary) while commuting to classes at New York University in 1937. These tickets were not considered unusual or unique to the Railroad by either the author or his friends, something that may have been the result of youthful egocentrism, but which suggests that other metropolitan railroads with considerable commuter traffic probably also sold such discounted tickets. Very few primary, and relatively few secondary, students traveled to class by rail, and the former would have been eligible for children's low-priced fares. Thus the "student" rate was aimed almost entirely at a substantial number of college age commuters and a limited number of young people attending private or specialized secondary schools.

The noted business historian N.S.B. Gras (1942) pointed out that the Harvard Co-operative Society, one of the earliest and most successful college bookstores, was founded in 1882 by a group of socially minded students who felt that their less affluent classmates should have some relief from the high prices charged by Harvard Square merchants. Gras, in turn, attributed the retailers' high prices to three factors:

1. The seasonality of their business since summer school offerings and enrollment were very small.

2. A monopoly position that resulted from the students' reluctance to travel to lower-priced downtown stores.

3. Widespread credit abuse on the part of both Harvard students and faculty.

DISTRIBUTION

Fallows (1901, p.165) noted that "confectioners, bakers, photographers, dry-goods merchants, tailors, and hundreds of others" use students as middlemen to reach the "inside college public." Many present day organizations such as American Airlines (Alexander 1990) and Koss (Day 1989), a maker of headphones, use students as on-campus representatives to sell to the college market. College bookstores have long represented a major outlet for textbooks, supplies, and college insignia garments (Goss 1988; Gras 1942). Spangles, described earlier, was distributed through college bookstores (Dumont 1929). Cooperative high school stores also emerged as a channel to youth (Nemetz 1939). Clearinghouses distributed educational material which could also be obtained directly from a vendor (Palmer and Schlink 1934).

Retailers located in college towns frequently catered to the college market. Credit, packaging, pricing, and sales force training advice for small, college-town clothing establishments was offered by Burns (1929). Detailed spending patterns were provided by Yocum (1934), who estimated, for example, what proportion of total clothing expenditures by Ohio State University students was spent in Columbus clothing stores.

RETAIL SECTIONALIZATION

The sectionalization of apparel on the basis of gender and child versus adult has long been practiced in department store retailing. A more recent event is the sectionalization of apparel for the intermediate age group within each gender. Jacobson (1928) discussed the need to differentiate the lines and advertising of older boys (those between 15 and 18 years of age) from those of younger boys (those between 8 and 15 years of age), and stated that "placing all boys from age 8 to 18 in one group is an unsound practice" (p.10). He provided two reasons for sectionalizing. Quoting budget studies (also see Nystrom 1929), he stated that older boys represent only 18.6 percent of the male population between the ages of 8 and 18, but account for 35.4 percent of clothing purchases made by or for boys between the ages of 8 and 18. Second, he noted the marked differences in styles, tastes, and needs between boys over and under 15 years of age.

In their case book on retail distribution, McNair and Gragg (1930) presented layout plans of several department stores. One layout of a 1924 women's floor (p.152) shows distinct sections for misses' dresses, suits, and coats. Another layout of a 1925 women's floor (p.159) shows distinct sections for misses' coats and misses' inexpensive dresses, as well as a women's "college shop." Neither case study was concerned with whether the youth sections should exist. Lord and Taylor operated a fourth floor "youth" department in their New York outlet (Sinsheimer 1926, p.71). As well, a number of retailers during the 1930s operated sectionalized youth apparel departments (Gillespie 1990). An unidentified menswear retailer was reported in 1933 to have created a special shop for high school students, distinct from the younger boys' area. This shop was decorated with pictures of the varsity sports in which the local schools engaged (Lyons 1933). It is not clear whether the idea of the separate shop itself or the decoration was the innovative point being held up for other merchants to emulate, but we suspect that both were regarded as noteworthy.

The *1933 Departmental Merchandising and Operating Results for Department Stores and Specialty Stores* (NRDGA Controllers' Congress 1934) included profits, gross margins, and turnovers for separate juniors' and misses' coats and suits, and dresses departments, but not for any sort of young men's department. At least as early as 1930, NRDGA recommended a uniform departmentalization and accounting system that fanned out to treat misses coats and suits and misses dresses separately from comparable women's garments and junior's and girlswear (Schacter 1930).

Not all merchants moved swiftly toward youth segmentation. Robert Kahn, a consultant with a long retail background and memory, recalls that when he was affiliated with Smith's of Oakland, California (the largest men's and boy's store west of Chicago), in the late 1940s, the firm suddenly realized that it was not obtaining the patronage of young men who were making their first clothing purchases "on their own." Parents apparently liked Smith's because of its reputation for quality, but the youths preferred competitive stores that had established stronger assortments in styles with more appeal to their tastes. Smith finally responded by opening a "Varsity Shop" to draw the youth market around 1948 (Kahn 1988).

Department stores had long segmented on other bases. In 1910, for example, Rich's of Atlanta opened its Economy Basement Store for low income and price sensitive consumers while selling its highest fashion clothing through private showings in exclusive (i.e., expensive) departments. They also coordinated their merchandising and promotional activities with the social calendar (Baker 1953, p.112–8).

CHAPTER FIVE

Special Product Design

We have discussed special youth promotion, special youth pricing, and special youth distribution applied to a wide range of products such as automobiles, apparel items, personal hygiene products, typewriters, and cigarettes, and services provided by such establishments as hotels and inns, dance halls, and barber shops. "Romance, dress, athletics, dancing, movies, motoring, and other recreations" provide a partial list of interests which "begin at puberty and increase in intensity until the age of perhaps thirty" (Wheeler 1924, p.165). Some businesses by their very nature tend to be age specific. Among physicians, pediatricians, obstetricians, and gerontologists tend to see different groups of patients. In this chapter we will look at some particular youth-

TABLE 5.1
Median age at first marriage: 1890–1970

	Year								
Gender	1890	1900	1910	1920	1930	1940	1950	1960	1970
Male	26.1	25.9	25.1	24.6	24.3	24.3	22.8	22.8	23.2
Female	22.0	21.9	21.6	21.2	21.3	21.5	20.3	20.3	20.8

Source: *Historical Statistics of the United States, Colonial Times to 1970: Bicentennial Issues, Part 1* (1975), Washington, D.C.: Government Printing Office.

oriented trades and product classes to see examples of special product design.

BRIDAL TRADE

Wedding-related businesses tend to be age oriented. Weddings can occur at any age, but between 1880 and 1940, first weddings—the one usually associated with the most elaborate celebrations and the most extensive gift-giving—tended to cluster during or near the years of youth, especially for the bride. As seen in Table 5.1, median age at first marriage remained below 22 for females between 1890 and 1970, but more or less declined for males between 1890 (median age of 26) and 1970 (median age of 23).

Many vendors, of course, sought this lucrative market.

Just consider, for instance, the businesses and services and professions that feel the repercussions of a wedding: florists, caterers, photographers, bootleggers and police [apparently rewarded to ignore the bootleggers] are only the most obvious. Think of the dress-making industry, the great department stores, the modistes, the milliners, the wholesalers and retailers and importers.

. . . The wedding is the symbol of even further ripples in the commercial pond. Think of the advertisements scanned, the stock of furniture researched [by the bride and groom] (Vincent 1925, p.96).

Parenthetically, the author of this 1925 quotation wondered whether his imaginary model couple had thought out the problems of "modern" marriage, including those of a two-career family.

Back on the selling side, an odd little retailing handbook (Lyons 1933) told retailers how they could copy a dozen or so other merchants in attracting bridal trade. Most of the suggestions involved a free gift to the bride or a beauty contest in which store patrons voted among photographs of June brides outfitted by the store (we wonder how much business was subsequently done with customers not voted beautiful or if the counting was biased toward those who spent the most money in the store). One merchant maintained a list of gifts already selected for each bride—a means of avoiding duplication and a rudimentary bridal register.

SPORTING GOODS AND ATHLETICS

During the second half of the 19th century, interest in both gymnastics and athletics was fostered by many groups. Athletic clubs, German gymnastics societies, Scotch Caledonian clubs, and professional sporting teams all contributed to the popularization of physical exercise as did the culture that made well-being a personal and moral duty. Many writers within the physical education movement urged increased exercise. "It was the rise of intercollegiate athletics, however, that insinuated the new craze into every crevice of the national consciousness" (Park 1989, p.145).

The endorsement of collegiate athletes is obviously useful in promoting sporting goods. A.G. Spalding, one of the earliest and most successful aggressive sporting goods marketers, successfully used the endorsement of intercollegiate associations such as the American College Baseball Association and the Intercollegiate (football) Association in declaring his baseballs and footballs to be "official." Similar recommendations from many of the professional clubs also helped foster sales. Spalding published numerous guides and manuals as promotional devices and advertising mechanisms, including *College Athletics* (cited by Park 1989, p.144). The manufacturers tended to offer goods at a wide variety of price ranges so as to appeal to all market segments, from the sandlot juvenile players to the professionals and well-to-do or well-supported amateurs (Hardy 1990).

The role of college women in innovating both the practice of participation in sports and the wearing of active and spectator sports apparel in the 1890s is cited by Banner (1983, p.7) as a contradiction of Veblen's trickle-down theory of fashion behavior. She attributes the movement more to the institutions' own innovativeness and their response to medical articles on student health. The claim that fashion originates at many levels other than the peak of the pyramid is long familiar to marketers; this collegiate evidence supports that position, but must be observed in context. In general, students, and especially female students, at the end of the 19th century were drawn almost completely from the more affluent and influential sections of society. Also in viewing student influence, the question must be asked as to which students were involved. For example, in the early 1940s, one of the authors of this paper was taught that college students were extremely influential in setting men's fashions, but that "students" in this sense should be defined as members of selective eating clubs at Harvard, Yale, and Princeton, and for winter sports clothing only, Dartmouth.[2]

Banner (1983) pointed to the interest in sports of "young aristocrats" a hundred years ago and to their later influence in adopting

2. Author's recollection of Mr. Henry L. Jackson's lectures in the class 'Merchandising Men's Fashions,'' New York University School of Retailing 1941: at the time Jackson was the men's fashion editor of a leading trade magazine, and of *Collier's Magazine*, and a well-known fashion consultant.

a more sensual style of dress. Yet it must be noted that the student body was more heterogeneous than the Social Register, and Banner's point is well taken.

At least as early as the 1890s, bicycle suppliers showed in their ads young, unmarried, and unchaperoned couples pleasantly cycling—and enjoying some courtship advantages (Green 1986, p.227). A 1920s ad for Kelloggs Shredded Krumbles that showed a young woman tossing a basketball said the product "is the real energy food" (p.229). Green, in his book on fitness in America, was of the opinion that dietary groups were among the first to support vigorous athletics for women. And during the 1920s physical fitness and health food advocates supported a more equal position for American women in society, even if most dietary reformers saw it mainly as a vehicle to prepare women for the traditional role of mothers. With respect to skiing, Donovan (1938, p.29) noted: "athletically inclined adults will probably take it up in increasing numbers, but the main body of the army of skiers will always be of school and college age." Morgan (the Montreal retailer now called The Bay) identified three categories of male skiers: (1) the beginner youth (or possibly man); (2) the proficient, but not expert, skier; and (3) the expert skier (of any particular age) who could be split into those preferring Norwegian skis and those preferring Swiss or Austrian skis (*Bulletin NRDGA* 1938b). The Morgan merchandising strategy apparently called for persuading the beginner youth skier to purchase low priced domestic skis and the expert skier to purchase high priced imported skis. Many ski garment ads featured youthful models (see *Bulletin NRDGA* 1938c). And the "Snow Trains" of the 1920s and 1930s which were often day-trip ski package tours that included all or parts of train tickets, food, and lift tickets probably appealed primarily to the younger set.

MILITARY TRADE

In overcoming a reputation for being less masculine than pipe and cigar smoking, "World War I doughboys' approval of cigarettes in their rations gave cigarette smoking a patriotic endorsement" (Smith 1990, p.29).

During World War II, military personnel were the objects of special marketing efforts. Here again the group was composed of more than youth, but was heavily weighted toward the youth sector. The efforts were of two kinds. First, there were marketers that tried to have brand name creature comforts (soft drinks, beers, candy bars, cigarettes) distributed to military personnel, in part to obtain sales but also to build goodwill and brand preference. Coca-Cola installations, for example, were located wherever the military were (Tedlow 1990, p.61–4). Reduced transportation, movie admission, and similar reduced prices on other goods and services were also goodwill-building and distributive justice efforts, as well as attempts to sell marginal capacity at the lower end of the income scale without disturbing the general price level. The other approach involved the sale of gift items for the military and is exemplified by an article that advised department stores to set up military gift shops (Hanson 1940).

APPAREL

The copy in a "Mashie Hat" ad said, "this new soft hat was designed by us for young men—college men in particular" (*Printers' Ink* 1904a, p.42). Lord and Taylor sold "Youth's Suits" meeting the requirements of the "young man" (Sinsheimer 1926, p.71) (from the drawing accompanying the ad, the young man appeared 20 or so). And the Hart Schaffner & Marx style books mentioned earlier also indicate that specialized apparel was designed for young men or youthful-minded adult males.

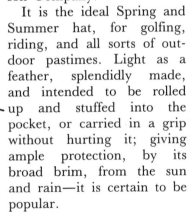

The appearance of special teenage *misses* dress styles and sizes has already been noted. These garments very much resembled women's styles, but were often somewhat simpler, made of lightweight material, less matronly in cut, and more reflective of the girls' interest in sports, parties, and dancing (Paoletiff and Krelogh 1989, p.34). A standard size range developed by the first decade of the 20th century, and the importance of that range increased as teenage spending power grew. Special styles for adolescent males developed somewhat later (Paoletiff and Krelogh 1989, p.34).

A 1939 report describes how many department stores discovered that age, style, and size considerations did not necessarily coincide in segmenting their female ready-to-wear market. A commercially relevant number of large-dimensioned young women were trying to patronize the age-appropriate misses department in spite of the inadequacy of the maximum size 20. The stores were trying to persuade manufacturers of misses lines to extend their size range. At the same time, the customers whose age was more appropriate to the women's department divided between those who wanted youthful and those who wanted matronly styles. Size was again a problem since some of the older or more conservative women had slim figures. The solution of choice seemed to be to divide the women's department on the basis of style with relatively full size ranges in both categories (although that would require fairly substantial stocks). The discussion assumed that all stores would have a separate misses department (*Bulletin NRDGA* 1939).

Most of the style and dress accoutrements of the 1920s' ''flaming youth'' or flapper are attributed by Fass (1977, p.280–6) to the initiative and authority of collegiate youth. These include the short skirt, tubular dress, silk stockings, bobbed hair, increased use of makeup, and the discard of various layers of undergarments on the part of women, and the greatly increased use of hair and facial lotions by men. To some extent, there was a unisex movement since young women adopted male vests, neckties, and knickers.[3] Male use of facial powder and similar preparations was borrowed from the female gender.

It is obvious that while students could have and undoubtedly did popularize these clothing trends, they were really in no position to originate, produce, distribute, or commercially promote them. Fass does note (p.126) that the style-setting power of the college youth was enhanced and exercised through commercial institutions such as movies, newspapers, and advertising. Some of these agencies must be considered as "third party" participants in the marketer–consumer dyad. The movie about college life (which she cites as a new genre) was not the creation of specific product manufacturers, although it represented a way in which movie producers could profit from attention to youth, and probably drew many youths to the movie houses. But the manufacturers and their distributors themselves obviously were oriented toward the youthful tastes. Fass mentions the particular case of silk stockings which became important in an era of short skirts. They were available in a wide range of colors, weights, and exotic cutout designs, which seems to suggest considerable attention to consumer tastes on the part of the hosiery industry. More astonishingly, she claims that they seem to have become a suitable product for a young man to give to a young woman. The "mamma's boy" conservative type might still consider a volume of Tennyson's poems more appropriate, but not the socially aggressive figure.[4]

---

3. We use the word "knickers" in the American rather than British sense. In American English it refers to informal, short cuffed, loosely fit trousers or pantaloons terminating just below the knee, typically worn by men and boys for sports. A particularly baggy style popular for golfing was known as "plus fours." In British English it refers to an article of female undergarments.

4. The more elderly of the two authors of this book was not old enough in the 1920s or even much of the 1930s to think of giving a young lady a present except perhaps at an adult-supervised birthday party. The 1930s were a more restrained period than the 1920s, but he does not recall silk stockings as being considered an appropriate gift item except as part of mildly salacious movie or theatrical humor. This may only be an indication of a sheltered childhood.

Youth advisory boards were convened by apparel manufacturers and retailers (Schere 1941). The "University Style Advisory
Board," organized by the Knox Hat Company, was used to promote the firm's Dunlap line of hats. Board members were expected
to "assist the company with suggestions and criticisms in the selection of styles likely to meet with the approval and adoption of hat
wearers in their section of the country" (DeCamp 1929, p.102).
The board consisted of male students from Yale, Princeton, Michigan, Virginia, Washington, and LeLand Stanford. Members were
paid a salary and met twice a year in New York at the company's
expense, but no promotional work was expected of them once back
at college. The company prepared dealer window and counter
displays that emphasized the board's role, and special displays were
created for the area surrounding each of the student's educational
institutions. An envelope-sized folder for distribution to consumers
was also prepared that said:

> Dunlap has engaged the services of six students of six American
> universities to assist in styling Dunlap hats. These men know
> style, and Dunlap spring hats are fashioned to the ideal of the
> young man and the man who stays young. For over seventy five
> years Dunlap has been the choice of gentlemen.

A number of New York (and other) stores had college advisory
boards by the mid 1930s (Gillespie 1990). By 1940, the Flint and
Kent department store of Buffalo, NY, and E.T. Slattery of Boston
operated advisory boards for their college departments, respec-
tively having 8 and 18 members (Donnell 1940). These boards
were also, and in some instances, mainly promotional tools. They
were often treated as advertising and the department and specialty
store board members were frequently employed as part-time salespeople, particularly during the "back to school" selling season.
The store board members were usually personable and attractive
individuals who could draw a customer following from their own
schools and who might be seen as authority figures by new students
entering their schools. One of the authors of this book was involved

with a national teen-board (high school student) program in the 1960s, but by that time college boards had become passe.

MOVIES

In his book on the motion picture industry, Howard Lewis (1933, p.87), a marketing professor at Harvard University, said that "two factors which in general seem to have popular appeal [to moviegoers] are youth and beauty." But he felt their appeal had diminished with the advent of talking pictures. He also directly addressed the issue of segmentation (p.83):

> In the past the producers have said that pictures cannot be produced for particular classes of people. It has been their contention that these classes are too limited in number and that no picture created for a special class would have sufficient drawing power to make a financial success. Recently, however, more serious attention has been given to the problem and a few attempts have been made to produce pictures intended to appeal to particular classes of audiences. On the whole these have not been very encouraging. It is highly probable, however, that the reasons for this lack of success are to be found in the unduly high production cost of the films [lack of scale economies] and in the poor advertising they received. This problem of stratification is merely one of the difficulties confronting those responsible for the planning of the motion picture product.

Lewis also described how studios gauged public taste and preference. These methods included box office receipts, movie reviews by critics and trade papers, volume of fan mail, impressions gained from informal mingling with movie audiences, and informal feedback from film distributors and exhibitors. During the 1920s and 1930s, the motion picture business was one of the fastest growing in America. It was not until saturation was reached during the late 1930s and early 1940s, and especially until the advent of television and night baseball and football as competitors, that motion picture executives seriously considered the need for empirical market studies addressing audience composition and preference (Allen and Gomery 1985; Handel 1950). In some instances, research conducted during the 1940s supported long held notions that motion picture executives had from experience, principally that movie going was more popular among youth than among other age segments. Producers and directors, being creators of an artistic product, may have seen formal market research as an infringement on artistic expression, and may have been dissuaded from using research tools.

Age, in fact was the single greatest predictor of movie attendance. The results of several studies are presented in Table 5.2. The first shows that the age—attendance relationship is more or less independent of education level among women, and the second shows that it is independent of gender. Similar findings were reported within the British movie-going public (Abrams 1946). The fourth study summarized in Table 5.2 shows that preference for single features increased with age, while preference for double features declined with age. These studies were conducted during the 1940s, and industry sources suggest that they were among some of the earliest formal market research studies conducted on movie audience attendance and preferences. Extrapolating the results backward in time does present major problems. During World War II, many theaters discounted ticket prices which may have led to an increase in movie popularity among youth, and the proportion of youth serving in the military may also have skewed the results.

Gender was an important demographic variable to movie audience researchers. It apparently had little affect on movie attendance, but it did affect theme preference. For instance, males were more likely than females to prefer war films, but females were more likely than males to prefer love stories (Handel 1950).

Paul F. Lazarfield, who has been called ''one of the greatest social scientists of this century,'' (Fullerton 1989, p.319) was influ-

TABLE 5.2
Movie research and age

Percent attending movies at least once a week

	High school education	
Age group	yes	no
under 25	69	69
25–44	40	42
45 and older	31	11

Note: survey results of women in a Midwestern city reported by Lazarfield (1947, p.162).

Proportion (%) attending movies
number of times per week

Age group	0	1	2–3	3–4	over 5
Men:					
15–20	9.2	10.7	21.8	27.2	31.0
21–35	32.4	17.9	20.8	17.6	11.4
36–50	54.4	15.6	18.2	8.3	3.4
over 50	73.4	12.7	8.3	3.7	1.9
Women:					
15–20	15.6	8.2	23.8	27.5	24.9
21–35	35.8	19.1	22.3	15.1	7.6
36–50	51.5	18.8	16.5	9.6	7.6
over 50	72.8	11.4	9.3	5.8	0.7

Note: results of a 1947 survey of Des Moines, Iowa, citizens reported by Handel (1950, p.103).

Proportion of age group attending movies yesterday

Age group	15–19	20–29	30–39	40–49	50–59	60 and over
Percent	27	16	11	8	9	6

Note: results of a 1945 study reported by Link and Hopf (1946, p.116).

(continued)

TABLE 5.2

Movie research and age (*continued*)

| | Preference (%) for single and double features | |
Age group	Single features	Double features
6–11	23	77
12–17	42	58
18–24	60	40
over 24	68	32

Note: results of a 1940 national survey conducted by the American Institute of Public Opinion reported by Handel (1950, p.131).

ential in the movie audience research field. By 1947 (p.106), he said:

> The decline of frequent movie attendance with increasing age is very sharp. No other mass medium shows a comparable trend. This is probably due to a variety of factors. Movie-going is essentially a social activity, as we shall presently see, and young people are more likely to band together for the purpose of entertainment. Then, for the movies one has to leave the house, which probably becomes more distasteful as one grows older. Finally, radio programs and reading material offer a greater variety of choices, and each age group can select from these media items that interest them. The supply of movies, however, is much smaller and variety is more limited, and they are patterned to the tastes of younger people.

These audience research studies were distinct from psychological research sponsored by the film industry to address the fears of censor proponents such as women's and religious groups and other socially minded organizations. The impressive *Motion Pictures and Youth* monograph series had some well-known contributors such as L.L. Thurstone (Peterson and Thurstone 1933). The objective of the series was to investigate the effects of movie exposure on youth (in some cases, their definition of youth was somewhat younger than the group we are interested in). Shuttleworth and May (1933), for instance, addressed whether movie-attending junior high school-aged youth had different attitudes than non-movie-going youth toward crime, justice, sex, minorities, religion, religious figures, and foreigners, to name a few.

Starting in 1912, the Balaban & Katz organization built deluxe movie houses in secondary shopping districts and then in the Loop in Chicago. To accommodate young parents (or more precisely, parents of young children), these movie houses were equipped with attended nurseries where infants and children too small to attend the film could be left. Incidentally, the Balaban & Katz organization also anticipated many of the crowd control techniques for which the Walt Disney organization is now celebrated, moving lines of people through elaborate reception halls and salons to minimize their impatience with the waiting process (Gomery 1990).

Music

Currently, age predicts music preference better than any other demographic segmentation variable including gender and income (Goldblatt 1990). But standard histories of popular music in America (Hamm 1979; Ewen 1977) do not mention any special youth orientation in the late 19th century. Many of the tunes that were played and sung by young people were family favorites, such as "Sweet Adeline." Some of these were lugubrious, non-aphrodisiacal tunes such as "Mother's in the Express Car Up Ahead" (a tear-jerker recital of a small orphan's sad conversation with a railroad conductor).

But by the early 20th century, new music and new musicians began to appeal to at least subsegments of the adolescent and youth market. The popularization of jazz and syncopation (lewd rhythmic dancing) within the white culture can partly be attributed to the "flaming youth" of the 1920s. The *Photoplay Magazine* (1922) study reported that the 18–30 age group accounted for 48 percent of all phonograph and record purchases, while constituting 23 percent of the 1920 U.S. population (refer to Table 2.1). Indeed, one retailer recalled that:

> Manufacturers are even putting out a duet bench with the player piano, and it helps sell more of the pianos because two of the young people can use it (*Photoplay Magazine* 1922, p.35).

While many markets for musical recordings of one type or another declined during the Depression, the continued sales of "hot dance" albums recorded by popular black bandleaders like Duke Ellington and King Oliver were primarily the result of strong demand by collegiate youth (Sanjek 1988, p.72). In 1934, RCA began selling inexpensive record player attachments (priced at $16) that played music through radio sets. According to Sanjek (1988, p.127), the "youthful market," influenced by newly introduced swing music heard over late-evening radio broadcasts, soon accounted for 40 percent of sales.

"Crooners" also made a strong impression in the adolescents and younger youth of the 1930s. Mounted police were called out to control zealous youth during 1929 New York concerts by Rudy Vallee and the Connecticut Yankees (Ewen 1979), which predated Frank Sinatra youth pandemonium by thirteen years.

Muzak, which first piped in music to New York restaurants and hotels over telephone lines in 1936 (Goldblatt 1990), seemingly became quickly interested in age-based music preferences. An empirical study they conducted for a large East Coast insurance company in 1945 revealed that the popularity of swing-jive and popular dance music decreased with age (Spears 1947, p.19). For example, 63.4 percent of those aged 18 to 25 liked swing-jive music, while only 11.6 percent over the age of 50 expressed a similar attitude. The same study also reported that the popularity of semiclassical,

classical, waltz, polka, folk dance, Hawaiian, and hillbilly music increased with age.

In summary, the music and allied industries responded to perceived youth needs as early as the 1920s flapper era. The displacement of swing-jive with rock-and-roll as the music choice of youth was a repetition of an already observed process. Music and dance styles were developed that appealed to youth more than to the elderly. Just as the swing-jive music of the 1920s and 1930s became passe and reminiscent of a bygone era, so too has the 1950s music of Elvis Presley and the 1960s music of the Beatles. Coincidentally, the rock-and-roll era was heralded by the fact that, for the first time, the best-selling record titles in the United States were different from the best-selling sheet music titles (Hamm 1979).

Dance Halls

Dance halls and ballrooms attracted many young people (Fass 1977; Wirth 1928). Apparently, at least during the first decade or so of the 20th century, they did not cloak themselves in quite the same mantle of respectability and middle-class gentrification that the vaudeville theaters and movie houses were to adopt by the 1920s (Feiss 1990, p.113). They appealed primarily to working-class young men and women, they permitted unescorted females to attend as individuals or in groups, and they allowed dances that were considered rowdy or improper under prevailing conservative standards. Feiss (1990) seems to see them as drawing a type of still-respectable ''New Women,'' who sought liberation from immigrant or working-class family and job-related restraints, but wanted to achieve it through personal freedom and expression rather than through participation in good works or social movements.

In reviewing the whole range of commercial amusements that began seeking respectable female patronage at the turn of the century, Feiss (1990, p.114) concludes:

Clearly, leisure entrepreneurs were not an undifferentiated mass
in their handling of the 'women question.' Social division of
age, race, beauty, ethnicity, and class segmented the market for
leisure, and businesses carved out different pieces of it that required varying responses to the shifting relations of gender. [em-
phasis supplied]

MAGAZINES

In a 1929 book, Christine Frederick, a well-known home economist
who had become a prominent marketing consultant, said that the
leading women's magazines of that day definitely claimed to be
edited for the under-35 consumers because their purchasing potential and receptiveness to innovation was so appealing to advertisers
(p.23–4). Frederick did not specify a minimum age, so we do not
know whether she felt the magazine sought the 16 to 22 year old
audience, which she saw as narcissistic and relatively impervious
to economy, logic, health, and even sanitation appeals, but very
interested in style, variety, personal adornment, fun, and excitement. It would definitely include the 22 to 28 year olds: the "Ro-
mantic Home Builders" who wanted change and innovation.
Many of the 28 to 38 year old "Alert Housewives" of her fourfold
classification were also welcome members of that audience.

Frederick (and apparently magazine publishers) regarded
those over 38 as too conservative to be targeted, although elsewhere
in her book she suggested that senior citizens newly liberated from
mandatory stodginess constituted a major market opportunity
(p.26). She also thought that women now (1929) tended to retain
"youthfulness" and even "girlishness" through marriage and,
perhaps, up to the birth of a second or third child (p.24).

Many of the juvenile magazines listed in *N. W. Ayer and Son's
American Newspaper Annual* (1882) can be cited as created primarily
for the youth, young teen, or childhood segments. For example,

Youth's Companion would best be classified as a pre-teen magazine. Other magazines like *Young Farmer* and *College Humor* may have appealed to many age groups, but were probably particularly attractive to youth. The *Bachelor of Arts*, first published in 1895, was read primarily by college men (Vance 1896); the very popular *True Story*, first published in 1919, and the movie fan magazines sought and promoted a young audience (Marchand 1985); and *Babies: Just Babies*, a short-lived magazine first published in 1932, was edited for young parents (Peterson 1964). The *Bachelor of Arts* utilized an advisory board of college men from 25 different institutions. Publishers continued to target youth markets during the 1940s and early 1950s with the appearance of such magazines as *Seventeen, Senior Prom, Varsity: The Young Man's Magazine, Teen Digest, Teen-Age Romances,* and *Young Love* (the latter two were comic books).

Paul Cherington (1924), director of research at J. Walter Thompson, described relationships based on empirical studies that linked economic strata and occupational specialty to magazine readership. The seeds of an objective application of segmentation research to the magazine and advertising industries can be seen.

Further Comments on Christine Frederick

In another classification, Frederick (1929) recommended dividing consumers into three age-related groups: young, middle-aged, and old. She then subsegmented the young into nine types: flapper, boyish, vivacious, demure, winsome, statuesque, feminine, conservative, and uninteresting (p.25).

She makes less use of these age segmentation approaches than one might expect from the emphasis in her book's introduction. She does, however, report a study of "young, married consumers" that she conducted for a client in the table silverware industry. The young matrons rejected the idea of acquiring silverware to provide heirlooms because they disliked what they had received from their mothers and grandmothers and did not want to impose their tastes on their own descendants. In terms that sound very current today, they are quoted as saying that they lead very simple, time conscious, mobile, servantless lives in small residences and consequently want unpretentious, easily maintained tableware (p.218). Another study of debutantes found that packaging is very important in cosmetic choice. Frederick says that this is partly explainable by the fact that the young women are ''still part child'' and partly by the fact that attractive packaging has general feminine appeal (p.194).

One of the most remembered ad campaigns of the 1920s was Palmolive soap's "That Schoolgirl Complexion" series. The box of copy in this ad states "Youth is charm, and youth lost is charm lost, as every woman instinctively knows."

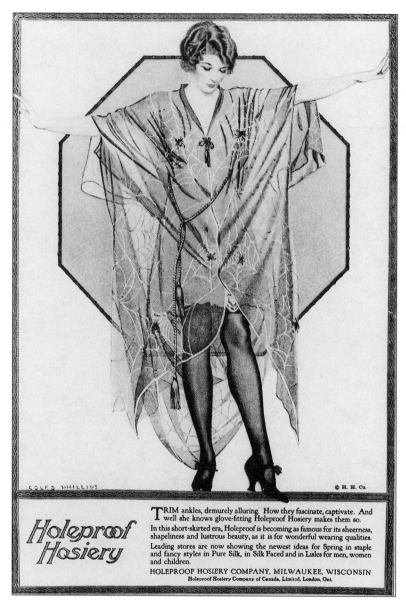

COLES PHILLIPS

© H. H. Co.

Holeproof Hosiery

TRIM ankles, demurely alluring. How they fascinate, captivate. And well she knows glove-fitting Holeproof Hosiery makes them so.

In this short-skirted era, Holeproof is becoming as famous for its sheerness, shapeliness and lustrous beauty, as it is for wonderful wearing qualities.

Leading stores are now showing the newest ideas for Spring in staple and fancy styles in Pure Silk, in Silk Faced and in Lisles for men, women and children.

HOLEPROOF HOSIERY COMPANY, MILWAUKEE, WISCONSIN
Holeproof Hosiery Company of Canada, Limited, London, Ont.

The image of a beautiful young "flapper girl" was used repeatedly in advertising during the 1920s and 1930s. These ads show how two different hosiery companies connected their products to the sexy, youthful image.

The kind of beauty that thrills

WOMEN have found that there's a most unusual kind of beauty about these Iron Clads—a fascination that holds your glance, and makes it hard to look away. It's not the kind of beauty which calls attention to the loveliness of the silk. But rather a mysterious quality which glorifies the wearer's own shapeliness and grace.

That is the kind of beauty that thrills. Nature's beauty. Beauty of form that's clothed in such a charming way that all its natural loveliness is revealed.

It's in the texture and the silk. And in that silk there's something else besides. There's Iron Clad wear—and wear—and wear.

ASK for IRON CLAD 907—$1.50 a PAIR.

Over 14,000 merchants are required to fill the great demand for Iron Clads. But if your dealer can't supply you, write us for Iron Clad 907—and we'll mail your hose direct. It's an exquisite sheer silk, full-fashioned style with silk to the hem, and a mercerized top and foot for extra strength. State size (8 to 10½) and color (black, white, gun metal, mauve taupe, French nude, grain, parchment, atmosphere, champagne, blonde, toast, woodland rose, silver grey, moonlight, skin, and peachbloom).

COOPER, WELLS & COMPANY
212 Vine Street, St. Joseph, Michigan
Mills at St. Joseph, Michigan, and Albany, Alabama

If you wish a seamless silk Iron Clad, ask for No. 806, $1.00 a pair.

Iron Clad Hosiery

G IT'S THE *YOUNGER CROWD* THAT SETS THE STANDARD!

O to the younger
crowd if you want the
right word on what to wear
or drive or smoke. And
notice, please, that the
particular cigarette they
call their own today is one
that you've known very
well for a very long time.

FATIMA

What a whale of a difference just a few cents make!

Fatima cigarettes were marketed to youth with copy such as this that was written in a 1927 advertisement.

John Held, Jr. illustrated this 1920 advertisement promoting Martha's Vineyard as a suitable travel destination for youth. He was well known during the 1920s for his cartoon-type ads depicting active young people in various situations.

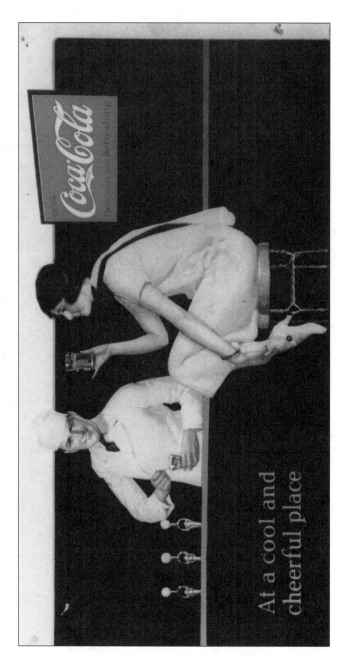

Early Coca-Cola advertisements established the product name as well as its place in society. In these mid-1920 ads, the soft dirnk is shown as a companion at "a cool and cheerful place" like the corner drugstore, where young people would meet, and is associated with youthful playfulness at the beach.

Somewhere West of Laramie

SOMEWHERE west of Laramie there's a broncho-busting, steer-roping girl who knows what I'm talking about. She can tell what a sassy pony, that's a cross between greased lightning and the place where it hits, can do with eleven hundred pounds of steel and action when he's going high, wide and handsome.

The truth is—the Playboy was built for her.

Built for the lass whose face is brown with the sun when the day is done of revel and romp and race.

She loves the cross of the wild and the tame.

There's a savor of links about that car—of laughter and lilt and light—a hint of old loves—and saddle and quirt. It's a brawny thing—yet a graceful thing for the sweep o' the Avenue.

Step into the Playboy when the hour grows dull with things gone dead and stale.

Then start for the land of real living with the spirit of the lass who rides, lean and rangy, into the red horizon of a Wyoming twilight.

The copy in this ad (circa 1925) for the Playboy automobile was one of the most successful pieces of writing to segment a product for youth. The young, carefree girl described in the advertisement produced a boost in sales for the Jordan car company.

Beautiful young women have been used to promote many products since the advent of advertising. In this 1933 ad for Hires Root Beer a later-day flapper girl enjoys the "delicious, healthful, economical" product.

HIRES is a registered trademark of Cadbury Beverages Inc., reprinted with permission.

Pre-World War I advertising introduced the country's young men to dress shirts with high, stiff collars. The long-running Arrow Collar Man campaign evolved into the Arrow Shirt campaign as collar-attached shirts became popular. Both campaigns featured college-aged, handsome Arrow male models.

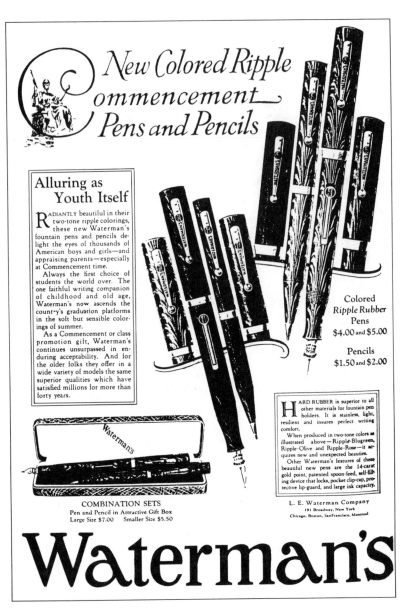

New Colored Ripple Commencement Pens and Pencils

Alluring as Youth Itself

RADIANTLY beautiful in their two-tone ripple colorings, these new Waterman's fountain pens and pencils delight the eyes of thousands of American boys and girls—and appraising parents—especially at Commencement time.

Always the first choice of students the world over. The one faithful writing companion of childhood and old age, Waterman's now ascends the country's graduation platforms in the soft but sensible colorings of summer.

As a Commencement or class promotion gift, Waterman's continues unsurpassed in enduring acceptability. And for the older folks they offer in a wide variety of models the same superior qualities which have satisfied millions for more than forty years.

Colored Ripple Rubber Pens
$4.00 and $5.00

Pencils
$1.50 and $2.00

HARD RUBBER is superior to all other materials for fountain pen holders. It is stainless, light, resilient and insures perfect writing comfort.

When produced in two-tone colors as illustrated above—Ripple-Blugreen, Ripple-Olive and Ripple-Rose—it acquires new and unexpected beauties.

Other Waterman's features of these beautiful new pens are the 14-carat gold point, patented spoon-feed, self-filling device that locks, pocket clip-cap, protective lip-guard, and large ink capacity.

COMBINATION SETS
Pen and Pencil in Attractive Gift Box
Large Size $7.00   Smaller Size $5.50

L. E. Waterman Company
191 Broadway, New York
Chicago, Boston, SanFrancisco, Montreal

Waterman's

The advertising copy for Waterman's pens touts the product as a gift that is "Alluring as Youth Itself." (circa 1927)

In 1902, Quaker Oats put forth an advertisement claiming its product deterred old age. While cosmetic companies strove to provide products to conceal aging, the cereal manufacturer claimed to actually "put off" the aging process by making "your blood tingle; nerves strong and steady; brain clear and active; muscles powerful."

McClelland Barclay illustrated this 1929 Texaco advertisement using, as was typical of his style, active, stylish, youthful figures.

This 1936 advertisement featuring the Jantzen Girl is an example of one of the best known youth-based campaigns. Historians credit the firm with introducing the term "swimsuit" to the American public and with encouraging the adoption of swimming as a leisure activity. This advertisement was illustrated by George Petty who also created the well-known Petty Girl during the 1930s.

Reprinted with permission, Jantzen Division of VF Corporation.

This 1917 poster is perhaps one of the most recognizable examples of military recruiting in the early part of the twentieth century. The ad, in fact, was so successful that is was used throughout both the first and second world wars to draw young people into the army.

CHAPTER SIX

The Cultivation of Youth by Nonprofit Organizations

Many nonprofit institutions singled out youth as a distinct public requiring special cultivation. In 1919, the Swiss federal government, for instance, ran an advertising campaign in New York, Philadelphia, and Chicago newspapers. Separate themes were used to attract tourists, businesspeople, and students. The tourist ad stressed aesthetic and health benefits, the business campaign stressed location and the ease of reaching major European capitals, and the student ad stressed educational benefits and the quality of Swiss libraries and educational institutions. The ads invited interested parties to write for more information to the New York office of the Swiss Federated Railroad (a public institution), and to identify their area of interest. In this manner, each target

EXHIBIT 6.1
Literature summary:
Youth marketing by nonprofit institutions (1880–1940)

Topic	Selected citations (alphabetical order)
Churches	Case 1921; Elliott 1920; *Literary Digest* 1926; Smith 1915
Colleges and universities	Elliot 1932; Elsworth 1899; Marts 1932; McJohnston 1916; *Printer's Ink* 1904b, 1904c, 1905b, 1917b, 1920b, 1920c, 1923a, 1923b; Quiett and Casey 1926; Robinson 1924; Smith 1915; Titus 1935
Public school support	Alexander and Theisen 1921
The military	Dickinson 1919; Keeler 1919; *Printers' Ink* 1917a, 1919a, 1919b, 1919c, 1919d, 1919e, 1919f, 1919g, 1919h, 1919j, 1920a
Public libraries	Johnson 1920; Wheeler 1924, 1935

market was sent brochures and booklets specifically designed for them (*Printers' Ink* 1919i). The Swiss, in fact, segmented the market on a benefits-sought basis, but since students also tend to be younger than tourists or businesspeople, age segmentation was also employed.

In the following sections, we describe in more detail seven nonprofit institutions: the American YMCA, churches, colleges and universities, public schools, noncollegiate fraternal and sororial associations, the military, and public libraries. Relevant literature is summarized in Exhibit 6.1.

THE AMERICAN YMCA

In London during the spring of 1844, George Williams helped organize an ecumenical society which two weeks later adopted the name Young Men's Christian Association (YMCA). The function of the YMCA, as spelled out in its first annual report, was the "improvement of the spiritual and mental condition of young men engaged in houses of business" (Eddy 1944, p.5). So popular was the institution that, within a decade, branches had been established in Scotland, America, Canada, and elsewhere. Like present day branches, YMCAs were local and highly autonomous. At the end of the 19th century, a typical American urban YMCA sought to promote membership to emancipated Protestant youth (Hopkins 1951; Pence and Speers 1946). Membership growth in America at that time was attributable in part to the large migration of male youth to urban areas.

The YMCA offered many services to its members and was engaged in many charitable causes. Libraries and reading rooms were particularly popular, but their frequency in YMCAs declined in the 20th century as public libraries became more widespread (Zald 1970).

One activity that YMCA branches promoted was athletics. This had obvious implications for sporting goods suppliers. In 1856, the Brooklyn YMCA proposed a formal athletics program to allow individuals to attain "vital and practical godliness" (Eddy 1944, p.46). But it was not until the 1880s, however, that the YMCA was transformed into an athletics institution, mostly due to the efforts of Luther H. Gulick. He was an advocate of what Green (1986, p.215) called "muscular Christianity." The philosophy was based on the ancient Greek pagan belief that a healthy body means a healthy mind. Gulick was reported to have said that the Greeks could be excused because there was no Christ at that time. During the 1890s, he and other proponents of the philosophy apparently had few moral reservations with the near nude photographs assiduously distributed by the Prussian-born body builder

Eugene Sandow. Sandow assumed classic poses in the photographs and, in many, his only covering was a fig leaf. As Green (p.213) explained, ''Sandow's legitimacy as model of the human form was more than simple pinup sexuality: he was the best example of someone who had assumed positive control of his body.''

The ability of athletics to deflect young men away from a life of immorality became quite clear. ''Physical exercises give to energy and daring a legitimate channel, supply the place of war, gambling, licentiousness, highway robbery, and office seeking [politics],'' argued Thomas Wentworth Higginson in 1861 (Green 1986, p.215). He continued, ''It gives an innocent answer to that first demand for evening excitement which perils the soul of the homeless boy in the seductive city.''

The American YMCA not only promoted fitness and health among youth, but it also helped fuel the rise of the athletic culture in the United States. Many branches eventually came to admit boys and men. When the YMCA's first Boys' Department was organized in America in 1866, it was because ''building boys was better than mending men'' (Eddy 1944, p.46). The inclusion of other age groups was probably not all that painful since most of the association's physical facilities were not specialized to meet the needs of youth. The athletic focus continued through the 1940s. At that time, 54 percent of the approximate 1,300 U.S. branches operated physical education programs, and across the nation the YMCA operated 850 gymnasiums, 600 swimming pools, and 306 health service programs (Eddy 1944, p.48).

CHURCHES

During the early part of the 20th century, several books appeared on ''Church Advertising'' (Case 1921; Elliott 1920; Smith 1915). Authors advocated applying ''modern business practice'' to religious promotion. Case (1921) described the church's minister as the "general sales manager" (p.43) and the competition for young men as places where they hung out (the barber shop, post office), and not other churches (p.106). Elliott (1920, p.30) advised church promoters that "special appeals need to be made in your advertising of interest to young men and women." He also recounted one campaign by a church located near several colleges (p.32).

The advertising man of this church spent a solid year:

> studying the mode of living and work of these students, and at the end of that time had in operation an advertising campaign that has filled his church with students at every service.

According to *Literary Digest* (1926), Kansas City businessmen ran a full-page ad just before Easter, specifically designed to attract "flaming youth" to local churches by offering a "new thrill" in excess of those offered by joy rides, parties, the Charleston, and snappy music. Reaction varied from Reverend Stidger's declaration that it was a fine ad "written in the language understood by young people" to Reverend Birkhead's comment that it would "cause the youth of Kansas City to become disgusted with the Church" and that it was "abominable" (p.28).

Chautauqua Institution, a church-sponsored summer resort founded in the 1870s that spearheaded a turn-of-the century social and cultural movement, apparently did not particularly concentrate attention on youth. Nevertheless, it maintained a collegiate-style summer educational facility that offered as early as 1887–88 a business course along with programs in the arts, social and physical sciences, and theology[5]. In the early years there were boys' and girls' clubs that embraced older as well as younger children, but at some time prior to 1938 it established a college club and a high school club to appeal to those particular age and educational segments (*Chatauqua Institution* 1938; Irwin 1990). The Depression ultimately discredited American business stewardship over the economy and signalled a decline in the extent to which religious

---

5. Source: Chautauqua University Circular of Information: 1887–88.

institutions used business and marketing terminology in describing promotional activities (Pritchett and Pritchett 1990).

COLLEGES AND UNIVERSITIES

Elements of a marketing orientation were recognized by some commentators. Smith (1915, p.204) observed:

> The "product" of a cultural college or school which is not run for profit is education for students and satisfaction for those who support it. In other words, the college has for sale, to use the terms of commerce, education and satisfaction. The field or market for this product naturally are the young people in the vicinity of the school or those who belong to the denomination with which the college is affiliated, and the wealthy men and women who may be persuaded that they can get greater satisfaction and pleasure from putting money in the endowment which will support these institutions than from other investments.

Smith (1915) seems to have clearly understood that educational institutions "sold a product" to different markets or publics, each public driven by distinct motivations. The specific publics served by colleges were not wholly agreed upon. Parents of students, alumni, the general public, and government were the publics identified by Titus (1935). Parental influence in the choice of institutions for youth may have been much stronger than under present day circumstances (Smith 1915, p.209), leading to the possibility that messages were designed to influence parents in order to attract youth, the final consumer.

Hower's (1949, p.589–93) analysis of billings by N.W. Ayer & Son, a leading advertising agency during the latter part of the 19th and early 20th centuries, revealed that educational institutions advertised heavily and accounted for a sizable portion of agency billings. Schools and colleges, not including correspondence schools, accounted for 4.2 percent of total billings in 1877 (ranked 8th among 40 categories). This rose to 5.5 percent (ranked 6th) in 1921, but dropped to 1.5 percent (ranked 13th) in 1930. The decline in ranking during the 1920s is somewhat deceiving because of the phenomenal growth of the agency's automobile advertising. Nevertheless, total school and college billings by Ayer hovered at about the one-half million dollar mark through the 1920s. Educational advertising was sufficiently important that Ayer created a special department to handle educational promotion. The agency also offered special credit, allowing institutions to advertise in the spring, but pay for services in the fall when tuition fees were collected.

In an extensive and informed review of the development of advertising in the United States, Sherman (1900) included an analysis of the types of products and services advertised in *Harper's* magazine from 1864 to 1900. Very little advertising of educational services appeared before 1873, no ads appeared in *Harper's* between 1874 and 1880, and Sherman had difficulty attaining information about the year 1881. The number of advertisements for such services, programs, and institutions from December 1864 to October 1900 are shown in Table 6.1. It indicates little or no advertising until 1868, but fairly steady growth after 1884. During the 1890s, 28.9 percent of the ads appearing in *Harper's* were placed by educational institutions. The types of programs advertised were not specified by Sherman.

The Sherman (1900) and Hower (1949) analyses suggest that educational institutions represented a significant revenue source for magazines and advertising agencies. The increase in educational advertising can, in part, be attributed to educational administrators who felt that advertising was required: one 1930s' study revealed that only 4 out of 250 college deans felt college advertising was unnecessary (Elliot 1932). In addition, magazines such as the *North American Review (Printers' Ink* 1892, May 25, p.677) and the *Church Standard (Printers' Ink* 1896 July 1, p.42) promoted themselves as suitable media vehicles, counseled colleges on how to

TABLE 6.1

**Educational advertising appearing in *Harper's Magazine*:
1864–1900**

Date	Number of ads	Number of educational ads	Percent educational
Dec. 1864	11	0	0.0
Oct. 1865	5	0	0.0
Nov. 1866	21	0	0.0
Oct. 1867	30	0	0.0
Sept. 1868	20	2	10.0
Oct. 1869	35	0	0.0
Oct. 1870	21	0	0.0
Oct. 1871	30	0	0.0
Oct. 1872	20	0	0.0
Oct. 1873	7	0	0.0
1874–1880*			
1881**			
Nov. 1882	15	0	0.0
Oct. 1883	52	5	9.6
Oct. 1884	43	3	9.8
Oct. 1885	62	7	11.3
Oct. 1886	97	10	10.3
Oct. 1887	35	15	42.9
Oct. 1888	197	11	5.7
Aug. 1889	237	52	21.9
Oct. 1890	348	73	21.0
Nov. 1891	409	45	11.0
Oct. 1892	403	94	23.3
Oct. 1893	307	55	17.9
Oct. 1894	353	106	30.0
Oct. 1895	374	131	35.0
Oct. 1896	329	123	37.4
Oct. 1897	348	123	35.3
Oct. 1898	330	119	36.1
Oct. 1899	322	113	35.1
Oct. 1900	294	93	31.6

TABLE 6.1

Educational advertising appearing in *Harper's Magazine*: 1864–1900 (*continued*)

1860s	143	2	1.4
1870s	57	0	0.0
1880s	1,086	176	16.2
1890s	3,469	1,002	28.9

Source: Sherman, Sidney A. (1900), "Advertising in the United States," *Journal of the American Statistical Association*, 52 (December), p. 142.

Notes from Sherman: *   no ads appeared during these years
    ** not accessible

advertise for recruitment purposes and how to respond to ad-generated inquiries, surveyed the attitudes of deans on college advertising (*Printers' Ink* 1905b), and surveyed other magazines on the frequency with which recruitment ads appeared (*Printers' Ink* 1904b). Research also played a role. Northwestern University analyzed inquiries generated from recruitment ads over a six-year period to formulate policy regarding seasonal timing, size, format, copy, and related graphic considerations (McJohnston 1916).

According to *Printers' Ink* (1917b), a number of university presidents (Washington University, Northern Ohio University, University of Oregon, Tulane University) increased student recruitment advertising expenditures to offset the effects of the World War I draft. Thus the extent of youth marketing by colleges and universities is in part a function of potential student supply in relation to perceived norms and/or capacity.

College catalogues and brochures were also used for recruiting purposes. The late 19th and early 20th centuries marked a period of curricula reform, as established institutions began offering "practical" courses in agriculture, business, and engineering, in addition to traditional courses in the classics (Boorstin 1973). Many of the newer land grant institutions focused heavily on "practical" course material. A coeducational opportunity, as well, was another major selling point stressed in some college catalogues. The content of many catalogues surpassed a simple description of curricula and described a wholesome atmosphere (hopefully met by parental approval), suitable location, and affordable prices (e.g., Colby College 1891–2; Kansas University 1893–4; as well as many others in the Warshaw files).

Newspaper coverage was a component of colleges' overall promotional efforts that were to some extent directed to the general public, rather than to youth, parents, and government legislators. Quiett and Casey (1926, p.4) observed that for nonprofit institutions, including colleges, "the publicity man [or woman] is the reporter for an institution." They provided sample articles about colleges published in newspapers written by college publicists.

Near the turn of the century, the University of Michigan (Elsworth 1899) and the University of Nebraska (*Printers' Ink* 1904c) mailed ready-to-publish newspaper articles about scientific and other achievements to the major dailies in surrounding cities. Students from both schools were encouraged to write articles about themselves for their hometown newspapers. Nebraska offered 25 cents for each story, regardless of whether or not it was published. Publicity, however, failed to center exclusively on academic achievements. During the 1930s, 39 percent of college-related newspaper articles appearing in major U.S. dailies centered on sports (Marts 1932), a fact not well appreciated by college deans (Elliot 1932).

Student recruitment and publicity endeavors were distinct from alumni and friends of the institution fund-raising campaigns. Fund raising efforts were extensive and included personal pleas by college presidents (Cutlip 1970; 1971), newspaper and magazine advertising campaigns (*Printers' Ink* 1920b, 1923a, 1923b), and special promotions such as a "gift" brochure (Barker 1930). The John Price Jones Corporation was begun in 1919 and by 1935 had collected almost $750 million for philanthropic causes. Between 1920 and 1950, the corporation recorded donations to a base of 50 colleges and universities. The results show the success of higher

education institutions' fund raising campaigns. Total yearly donations to the 50 institutions averaged about $55 million during the
1920s, $42 million during the 1930s, and $62 million during the
1940s (Cutlip 1965, p.246).

The sum of their promotional efforts created a positive public
image for the educational institution, attracted students, impressed
politicians, fostered strong alumni bonds, and attracted donations.
Educational institutions were aware of distinct publics and used
special media and messages to influence the general public, potential students and their parents, alumni, and gift-givers.

PUBLIC SCHOOL SUPPORT

Public schools have aggressively used publicity methods to garner
support for increased financial funding, at least since the early part
of the 20th century. These campaigns were designed to create in
the public a favorable attitude toward tax increases for enhancing
teacher salaries or for providing capital for the construction of new
buildings (Alexander and Theisen 1920; Fratis and Arlett 1920;
Stetson 1920). In the process of describing public school support
publicity, Alexander and Theisen (1921, p.19) said:

> The public is not to be thought of as made up of so many individu-
> als. It is rather to be regarded as consisting of foci or rallying
> points about which individuals, having interests and desires in
> common, center. The members of any one of these groups are,
> to a large extent, to use Professor Giddings' designation, ''like
> minded,'' so far as their motive for opposing or supporting the
> campaign issues goes. The problem for the campaign manager
> and his staff is to locate these groups, to discover the basis for
> their opposition or support, and to work accordingly.

They then described the major publics that school publicists
encounter: illiterates; literates or those familiar with the English

language; women; heavy taxpayers such as bankers, real estate owners, and manufacturers; retired farmers, especially in smaller communities, as they typically oppose tax increases; families with school-aged children who have an immediate vested interest in education; workers who cannot leave their place of employment and who, therefore, must be reached at work; *young people* between the ages of 18 and 20 who will, at some future date, vote and influence tax rates; and school children. Some of the nine segments obviously overlap. Our point in providing the above list is to demonstrate that segment identification was considered important, and even in a relatively esoteric marketing application, at least for the early part of the 20th century, youth was included as a key segment.

NONCOLLEGIATE FRATERNAL AND SORORIAL ASSOCIATIONS

The 1870s and 1880s saw a flowering of fraternal groups in America. According to Schmidt (1980), these groups divided into two overlapping categories: mutual insurance organizations that emphasized sickness, accident, life, and funeral insurance, and social (mostly secret) societies that emphasized rituals, brotherhood, recreational, and benevolent objectives. By 1920, half of the American population belonged to one of these societies (p.3). The insurance or mutual benefit groups appear to have set 16 to 18 as a minimum age for membership, along with (according to Schmidt's directory description) a requirement of an ''ability to earn a livelihood.'' In the early 20th century, many of these organizations used a ''graded'' fee or assessment system in which those who joined before the age of 35 paid lower amounts than those who joined later. Some of these groups also had ''juvenile departments.''

By 1920, in spite of their overall growth, many of the social groups became concerned about recruitment and established youth auxiliaries. The formation of such auxiliaries by some organizations probably both inspired and pressured others to do likewise. Several examples of youth auxiliaries are presented in Table 6.2 along with their fraternal or sororial sponsor and founding date.

Adult organizations such as the YMCA and YWCA and church groups sponsored some of the steadily increasing growth in high school fraternities and sororities during the first half of the 20th century, although most of that activity was probably student initiated. The educational authorities and state legislatures were concerned, and in many instances those societies were banned. They may have been perceived as undemocratic (i.e., exclusive), which conflicted with the egalitarian goal of public education. And they may have been seen as a challenge to school administration authority. Channeled through external ties to alumni associations and collegiate Greek letter societies, high school associations often exerted intense peer pressure. They could impose dress codes (e.g., pins, rings, insignia clothing) and deportment codes on their members that could seem to rival teacher and administrator power. Nevertheless, by 1940 as many as 20 percent of the students in some suburban high schools were affiliated (Graebner, 1987).

MILITARY RECRUITING

The fact that the military as well as colleges and universities, fraternal orders, and religious groups were engaged in the effort to recruit youth in the 1920s is not surprising. What is impressive is that the military saw it as analogous to a corporate marketing campaign. The Navy, Army, and Marines each viewed the other two branches as competition, considered potential recruits as customers, and thought that they were selling a way of life in the forces (*Printers Ink* 1919c).

Although the World War I demobilization had stripped the Army of most of its enlisted strength, Secretary of War (then a

TABLE 6.2
Founding years of youth auxiliaries

Youth auxiliary	Fraternal/ sororial organization	Youth auxiliary founding Date	Source
Junior Knights of Peter Cleaver	Knights of Peter Cleaver	1917	p.182
Junior Daughters of Peter Cleaver	Knights of Peter Cleaver	1930	p.182
Columbian Squires	Knights of Columbus	1925	p.73
The Junior Lodge	Odd Fellows	1921	p.245
Order de Molay	Freemasons	1919	p.90
Job's Daughters	Eastern Star	1921	p.169
Rainbow Girls	Freemasons of Eastern Star	1922	p.211
Antlers	Elks	1922	p.44
Maids of Athena	Order of Ahepa	1930	p.223
Sons of Pericules	Order of Ahepa	1926	p.233
Order of the Builders	Freemasons	1921	p.58
Junior Catholic Daughters of America	Catholic Daughters	1926	p.64
Junior Catholic Knights of America	Catholic Knights	1929	p.64
B'nai B'rith Youth Organization	B'nai B'rith	1924	*

*Sinruer, H. R. (1990), archival consultant to B'nai B'rith, letter to Stanley C. Hollander, June 19. All other material is from Schmidt, Alvin J. (1980), *Fraternal Organizations,* Westport, CT: Greenwood Press.

cabinet position coequal with the autonomous Secretary of the Navy) Newton D. Baker envisioned a rather large standing Army (approximately 300,000 enlistees) that would provide its personnel

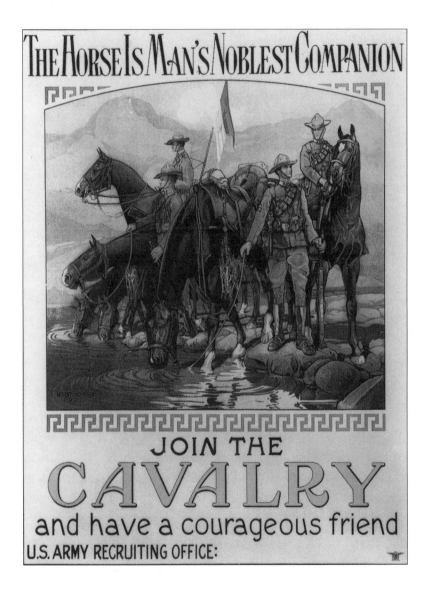

with educational and vocational training benefits. A large recruiting drive was undertaken during late 1919 and early 1920.

Floyd Keeler (1919), an Army captain who played a major role in developing and implementing the campaign, cited General Munson of the Morale Branch as saying:

> There will be a great deal of criticism of the Army now that the war is over and the officers and the men have had time to kick about the lack of promotion, poor food, getting back home, unnecessary drill, no leave and dozens of other things. . . . It is obvious that unless the public is adequately informed it will be next to impossible to obtain recruits for the regular Army in peacetimes.

A paid advertising campaign was mounted for the first time in the Army's history, urged on by an analogy with corporate practice (Griffith 1982, Chapter 2). The corporate analogy is not that surprising, since a principle author of the Army's formal recruiting strategic plan was an advertising man, Captain Roy Dickinson, who later became associate editor of *Printer's Ink*. Congress, however, decided on a much smaller force and appropriated pay for an even smaller annual average strength. Army personnel managers dampened the recruiting drive but tried to manipulate their efforts so as to have maximum effective forces available during the summer National Guard and Reserve training period (Griffith 1982).

As part of the plan entitled "Selling the U.S. Army to the Young Men of America," a Central Army Publicity Bureau was established in New York to "sell re-enlistment to soldiers now being discharged and enlistment to new prospects" (Dickinson 1919, p.65). In March of 1919, 32 Army recruiting branch chiefs attended a three day seminar in New York. Presentations were made by over 30 advertising experts including: Bruce Barton, one of BBDO's founders; J.D. Elsworth, advertising manager of AT&T; G. Fowler, advertising manager of Colgate and Company; and J. Sullivan, secretary of the Association of National Advertisers. Dingy recruitment offices in "seedier" city locations were abandoned and portable ones were erected at more favorable sites. The Publicity Bureau sent fliers to branch officers, educating them on how to overcome enlistment objections discerned from interviews with recently discharged soldiers (Dickinson 1919).

In the Army's official request for funding, regional recruiting officers were referred to as "regional sales managers" (*Printers' Ink* 1919d). The Secretary of War subsequently authorized $185,000 to be spent over a one month period to test the cost effectiveness of paid-for advertising (*Printers' Ink* 1919d).

A two-page ad was run in the newspapers of cities with a major Army recruiting office. The ad depicted Uncle Sam pointing out to a young man the educational opportunities and man-building abilities of the Army. The copy read "Suppose you are a young man looking about you for a trade as a stepping stone in life" (*Printers' Ink* 1919e). Because of the campaign's tight schedule, it was almost aborted when the Army realized that no form existed for requisitioning the services of a private advertising agency: a form used to purchase shoes, shirts, and sealing wax was ultimately used (Keeler 1919). A target of 50,000 new recruits was selected for judging the campaign's success; further consideration of paid-for advertising on a full time basis was based on their feedback (*Printers' Ink* 1919e). At the end of the campaign, over 100,000 enlistments were recorded, a striking success costing less than two dollars per recruit. This encouraged the Secretary of War to extend an additional $125,000 in funding for a follow-up campaign in smaller towns where recruiting substations were located (*Printers' Ink* 1919j, 1920).

The Army was not always a practical marketer. In 1925, a Major Philipson prepared an amazingly sophisticated, even impressionistic, report of the demographic and social attributes relevant to recruitment potential in each of the 56 geographic recruiting districts and many of their subareas. Griffith (1982, p.81), the recruiting historian, says that the report was forwarded to the Chief of Staff through the adjutant-general, but without endorsement or annotations and apparently without effect. The experience has not been unknown to modern marketing researchers. In the second half of the 1920s, Army personnel managers decided that emphasis on retention rather than recruitment was the answer to manpower problems, and so they successfully lobbied Congress for improvements in housing and rations.

Other military branches were also involved in recruitment and publicity drives. For instance, the Marines advertised for recruits (*Printers' Ink* 1919a), and Major Sterrett, who later became vice president of John H. Hawley Advertising Co., "trade-marked" the Devil Dog image of the Marines during World War I through an extensive newspaper publicity drive (*Printers' Ink* 1919b). And the Navy, shortly after World War I, conducted paid-for advertising recruitment campaigns (Harrod 1978; *Printers' Ink* 1919g) and newspaper and magazine publicity drives (*Printers' Ink* 1919c).

PUBLIC LIBRARIES

Public libraries were apparently quite willing to use regular library funds for promotional and advertising purposes (*Printers' Ink* 1927; Shannon 1921; Wheeler 1924). Hyers (1927) reported that public libraries in Buffalo, Cleveland, Detroit, and Los Angeles (as well as those in other cities) retained at least one full-time employee devoted to library promotion or publicity.

Librarians of the period seemed to have engaged in an explicit and implicit debate as to whether youth was the basis of reader segmentation, and, if so, whether it was an appropriate segment for their marketing and operational efforts. We will look at how some library experts consciously selected other basis for segmentation and positioning and even specifically rejected the youth market.

With respect to age segmentation, the distinction between child versus adult is critical since library facilities, services, and serial holdings for the child are distinct from those required to service adult patrons. For instance, Wheeler (1935) said that it was quite common during the 1930s for public libraries to create and distribute unique "how to use" manuals for children (of various ages) and for adults. Administrators of the Toledo Public Library, for all intents and purposes, segmented the market into child versus adult for promotional purposes and then further subsegmented the adult segment (Johnson 1920). They created distinct brochures and displays to attract specific adult publics (one of which was the professional businessman). Children were ignored, at least in this campaign, since administrators felt that they were already exposed to the public library through public school efforts.

In a very early use of the word segment, Wheeler (1935, p.375), in reference to an empirical study that split out the total market for one city's public library, said:

> The segment, "No desire for books," for example, might be as large as anyone wished to make it; its definition is elastic and it would overlap to some extent the 40 percent of prospective users.

His suggestions that a segment is elastic and that two segments may overlap are certainly intriguing. More importantly, library publicists were being urged to think of the market as composed of homogenous segments. We should note that Wheeler was no lightweight, having published at least five books on library administration spanning the 1920s to the 1960s.

In the spirit of a public institution, Wheeler (1935) felt quite strongly that, except in the case of holding "easy to read" books for the semi-literate or recent immigrant not fluent in English, public libraries should not favor the wealthy, the educated, or any other adult public in terms of services, facilities, or serial holdings. Aside from the moral grounds for adhering to such a belief, emerging empirical research conducted during the 1930s was demonstrating that literate adult reading preferences did not vary systematically with age, income, or occupational status (Gray and Monroe 1929; Waples 1934; Wheeler 1935). Reading preference is not synonymous with reading rate or library usage rate. Wheeler also felt it was common knowledge among library administrators that the relationship between age and library usage was U-shaped (1924, p.165–6):

> Because of these competing interests [romance, athletics, dance] . . . libraries unquestionably find a sudden falling off in the use of books, except as connected with school work, among girls and especially boys of 15 to 20, despite the perennial notion that teaching grade pupils to use the card catalog (sign of the library habit!) will make each succeeding wave of children into real book lovers.

Distractions probably increase for college students, and hence their partaking of public library services may decline even more.

We can speculate that the U-shaped relationship between age and library usage resulted in library administrators focusing their publicity efforts to children and adults, and to youth to a much smaller extent. In addition, at the upper end, library administrators may group youth with adults, the critical factor being their level of literacy. At the lower end, on the other hand, youth may be grouped with children, especially if they remain in grade school.

CHAPTER SEVEN

What Does All This Mean?

Our historical analysis of age-based segmentation led us to conclude that churches, colleges and universities, and the military to varying degrees adopted a corporate or marketing analogy during the 1920s. For instance, commentators urged individuals in these institutions to think of ministers and military recruiting officers as ''regional sales managers.'' Educational institutions sold knowledge to youth and satisfaction to benefactors, churches sold meeting places and salvation, and the military sold man-building and vocational training. And while we are unable to make any claim concerning who first introduced the word ''segment'' to marketing, our research revealed that a library administrator named Joseph Wheeler (1935) was a user before 1940. Marketing by non-profit institutions is perhaps an older practice than one might construe from a cursory glance at present day marketing textbooks.

Age is only one possible basis for segmentation. While all age categories are transitional, youth may be particularly seen as a stage of passage between two basic life states. Even the generous definition used here (15 to 24 years of chronological age) only encompasses a span of nine to ten years. A university president once described his college student daughter as being at that awkward age where she didn't know what wine to serve with the Twinkies (yellow cake filled with very sweet butter cream, popular with children). At the earliest years, youth certainly retains some of the characteristics of childhood or adolescence. At the upper bounds it takes much of the trappings of adulthood. Moreover, it is by no means homogeneous in all of its wants and needs. Besides allowing for personality differences and for variation in individual rate of physical, emotional, and intellectual maturation, youth also divides on gender, affluence, beauty, race, rural/urban, education, emancipation/dependency, and many other criteria.

Gelman (1990), drawing upon an unannotated comment of Todd Gitlin, suggests that modern teenagers are much less homogeneous in psychographics, if not in product choices, than their predecessors of the 1960s. But both logic and recollection indicate that youth, being human, has always been diverse, even in the 1960s, a position brilliantly demonstrated in Graebner's (1990) revisionist history, *Coming of Age in Buffalo*.

The reader will note the variations in the designation of the youth segment by different sources. Although we have concentrated on the 15 to 24-year-old group for the reasons we indicated in Chapter 1, some of the sources quoted use other breakdowns. Some authors and firms were particularly interested in college-age youth, others such as Mrs. Frederick (1929) and *Photoplay Magazine* (1922), discussed people up to the age of 30 or thereabouts. This ambiguity is natural and even informative. Some of the variation in age categorization is undoubtedly due to personal perception or to convenience in data collection. But some of it is also due to differences in commercial interest. Manufacturers and retailers of things for college consumption obviously wanted to adjust to one specific slice of society; others wanted to reach more of the people at family formation stages. Thus, we can see demonstrations of a sort of tailor-made segmentation adjusted to individual vendor needs.

Youthfulness or what might be called *youngness*—a nostalgic and fantasized state of looking and feeling young without having any of the cares and concerns that youth actually faces—has a strong appeal to many older and younger individuals. It is the basis for the *youth appeal* that has been used in much promotion to those markets. It is part of the "Pepsi Generation" campaign.

ATTENTION DEVOTED TO YOUTH

The material reviewed here does suggest that youth has been a theme of interest to Americans at least since the 1920s, and probably earlier. A recent novel, *The Final Club* by Geoffrey Wolff, deals with the experience of a young man who is rejected by all the desirable eating clubs (local fraternities) at Princeton. The *New York Times* weekday book reviewer, although liking the book in spite of finding many weaknesses of craftsmanship, was moved to ask: "Is Geoffrey Wolff kidding? Does he really expect his readers in this age of falling barriers to take seriously a novel about rejection by an eating club?" (Lehman–Haupt 1990, p.B2). The reviewer asked this question on the same day that his paper ran its weekly section devoted to campus life. He did not mention that in 1912 another novel, *Stover at Yale*, by Owen Johnson, which dealt with the exclusionary tactics of eating clubs at Yale, was a national best-seller and the subject of widespread discussion. Even though only a very small portion of the American population was then college-educated and only an infinitesimal proportion went to Ivy

League schools, collegiate youth were often a subject of interest. Just as youth, its morals, its tastes, and its prospects have been a major theme for laudatory and critical periodical articles, so, too, has the campus long been an important locale in American fiction. The latter is partially the result of the fact that a good portion of the novelists have obtained teaching positions as a source of income and are following their own advice to ''write about what you know best.'' The collegiate movie also became a staple in the early 20th century.

YOUTH MOVEMENTS

The tendency exists to think of each successive generation of youth as having unique features from those preceding it. The youth movement of the 1960s and 1970s had elements of uniqueness. They included the Vietnam War and its pictorial delivery to the American home, guilt feelings on the part of those who obtained academic deferments, the impact of the baby boom with the resultant growth in the proportion of youth exposed to college idealism, Dr. Spock's widely accepted philosophy of permissive child-rearing, and unusual prosperity.

The 1920s' ''flaming youth'' movement also had elements of uniqueness in its own right. The *Reader's Guide to Periodical Literature* for the mid-1920s contains a tremendous number of citations with such titles as ''Our Troubled Youth,'' ''What Is Wrong With Youth Today,'' and the like. Its uniqueness may have been the widespread adoption of the automobile, new music (swing–jive) and new dancing (syncopation), the expansion of colleges and universities (albeit not at the rate of expansion during the 1960s), or the end of the war, which resulted in the return from overseas of ''disillusioned'' male youth. The 1920s' youth may have been more self-centered, more consumption oriented, and rebellious in a very different way than the societally active 1960–70s' youth, but

"Roll Your Own!"

A fresh, hand-rolled cigarette of "Bull" Durham makes a smoke that's as lively and brisk as a pure-ivory billiard ball. "Bull" Durham has the alert, healthy, youthful taste—the snap and sparkle that give the "punch" to a cigarette. That's why so many more thousands of live smokers have become "roll-your-own" enthusiasts during the last few years.

GENUINE
"BULL" DURHAM
SMOKING TOBACCO

No other tobacco has the unique, mellow-sweet mildness and the delightful aromatic fragrance of "Bull" Durham. Made exclusively from mild, ripe Virginia-North Carolina "bright" tobacco leaf, "Bull" Durham has that distinctive quality which has made it the favorite smoke of three generations.

"Roll your own" cigarette with "Bull" Durham and get more genuine satisfaction out of smoking.

THE AMERICAN TOBACCO COMPANY

they did seem to have their own split with the older generation. The break between the older and younger generations during the 1920 and 1960 youth movements may have, in part, been the result of youth's shared cohort values and, in part, the result of youths' rebellious and reckless tendencies.

But regardless of the characteristics of a youth cohort group, and whether or not the younger generation coalesced into some sort of "movement," both profit and non-profit organizations, especially since the 1920s, have been willing to court them and to adjust their marketing mix to suit them. The evidence clearly shows that numerous vendors have selected youth or youngness as a basis for segmentation or positioning since at least the late 19th century. The "Pepsi Generation" definitely did exist before the Pepsi–Cola Company publicized the generation's birth announcement.

COHORT THEORY VERSUS YOUTH INFLUENCE

Youth as a habit setting cohort and youth as a collection of individuals that influence other age groups (mainly former youth) are possibly conflicting views. Our study was not designed to test their relative validity. We are able, however, to make some observations on these two theories.

We have noted some striking examples of the buying pattern molding role of youthful purchases cited in the literature. Yet we have also noted some of the striking signs of brand switching and personal behavior change on the part of older cohorts, often in response to pressure or stimulus from youths. For an example, take Wirth's immigrants who wanted to remain in the old-fashioned ghetto of their formative years, but who ultimately yielded to their children's desire for a more impressive address. At another level, take those older individuals who switched from Coca–Cola to

Pepsi–Cola as the "Pepsi Generation" eclipsed the "Coke Set" as a symbol of youthfulness.

Changes in product and brand choice are inevitable. Tastes (and even the physiology of taste buds) alter over time; life situations and needs vary; accumulating experiences provide disconfirmation as well as reinforcement of previous decisions and expectations; and a constant barrage of new messages from both commercial and noncommercial sources seeks to induce change.

It may well be that the entire general experience (the *gestalt*) of the youthful years has a profound influence on subsequent dispositions. Moreover, early product and brand choices, especially if frequently and satisfactorily repeated, will establish barriers, but by no means impervious barriers, to rival options. Simultaneously, the high value accorded to youthfulness in the American culture will give the decisions of subsequent generations considerable weight in overcoming these barriers. Thus "youth as habit setter" and "youth as exemplar" essentially are two competing vectors for consumer behaviorists to incorporate in their multi-causal models.

In an interesting twist, replaced youthful choices may return to the individual's buying agenda, after obtaining sufficient age and affluence to indulge in nostalgia (Sheth 1991). Nostalgia, by definition, is a desire to return to the past. That past may be one's own earlier years, as exemplified by recreational patterns in which individuals engage in trips or sports that were connected with their youth. For many, many years, Lionel successfully advertised that its toy trains were designed for "the man in every boy and the boy in every man." This was partially an appeal to the theme of family togetherness, but also way of suggesting to the fathers (who would make the purchase) that they could recapture childhood fun. Sociologists have noted that the grandchildren of immigrants (unlike children) very frequently exhibit a sentimental fondness for ethnic food and ethnic culture provided it does not interfere too much with their current way of life. Similarly, the nostalgia may be for a very vicarious sort of national youth as many people whose families arrived in the country at much later dates express a liking for

American colonial furniture or early American antiques. Thorsten Veblen expressed the though somewhat similar to Sheth's that the hardships of youth can become the luxury of later life when sufficient affluence has been attained. Thus dining by candlelight became a sign of elegance for people who in earlier stages of the life cycle were forced to do so.

DIFFICULTY AND EASE OF YOUTH MARKETING

Youth's image is not always positive. After World War II, the McDonald brothers, who built the first hamburger fast food establishment that bears their name, and Ray Kroc, who nurtured the McDonald's Corporation into a worldwide enterprise, took great pains to disassociate their drive-in establishment from the popular image of a "youths' hangout" widely associated with other drive-ins (Love 1986). Similarly, a well known advertising campaign of the 1950s for a male hairdressing (Brylcreem) held it out as an alternative to "greasy kid's stuff."

Positioning on a youthful dimension may be dangerous if the strategy alienates established, older customers. Recently, the Oldsmobile division of General Motors Corporation, perhaps seeking to replace a somewhat middle-aged image, mounted an extensive television advertising campaign that featured scenes of excited young people enjoying or admiring a sporty-looking car. These ads culminated in the catchy musical slogan: "This [the new Oldsmobile] is not your father's Oldsmobile." The ads scored well in surveys of consumer recognition and recall, but they did not sell cars (Treece 1990). In fact they seemed to induce resentment among older, loyal customers and workers, who felt repudiated by the implied criticism. This type of problem was apparently recognized by DeCamp during the 1920s:

Jazzing-up an old established product in an attempt to make it acceptable to college youth sometimes wins, not the college crowd, but imitators of it, and thereby loses the market aimed at and the one already possessed (1929, p.101).

The 1987 mini-skirt fiasco provides an additional example of the dangers inherent in youth positioning. Apparel designers and retailers pushed mini skirts and above-the-knee length skirts to girls and women in the casual, business, and top-tier apparel categories during the spring and summer of 1987. The link between the short skirt and youthfulness was undoubtedly understood by many designers and retailers. "Women are very happy with the shorter length because it makes them look younger" (Carolina Herrera, clothing designer interviewed by Conant and Wingert 1987, p.69, in *Newsweek*). But there was an upper limit to the skirt length acceptable to professional businesswomen. Conant and Wingert (1987) observed that older women who were young during the 1960s recalled "what it was like to be at the office without adequate camouflage" (p.70), and stated that designers were showing a "reckless disregard for age and dignity" (p. 69). Yet New York retailers were excited and apparently could not sell enough of the shorter, more modern looking skirts, at least to very young women (*New York Times* 1987).

By 1988 it was evident that professional women were not buying short skirts for the business place (in both the emotional and the dollar sense of the word), and that many women were not buying them for casual wear. Skirt hems certainly rose during this period, but nowhere near to the extent hyped by designers, retailers, and celebrity endorsers. In 1988, retailers scrambled to offer a choice of skirt lengths (and even pant suits), in some cases clearly labeling the skirt length in inches so that shoppers could identify length with ease. A spokeswoman for B. Altman & Co. (interviewed by Sloan and Graham 1988), said that they would offer short and long skirts, but not extreme in either case, and would stress short skirts in advertising copy. While the skirt lines offered by Altman appealed to a broad range of age groups, advertising would stress a youthful store image through short skirts. This apparently was not enough to change consumers' view of Altman's respectable, high quality stodginess. After many unproductive years, its main store and most branches were closed in 1990.

Part of the 1987 mini-skirt problem was that some designers and retailers failed to incorporate into their plans the long-understood notion that the junior market is composed of two over-lapping segments. Jan Cobb, a divisional merchandising manager at Rich's explained as follows (interviewed by Wallace 1988, p.53):

> You have what is really a better junior customer who is older and wears a junior size. And then you have the high school girl and the college girl who want what is new and different.

The younger, not the older junior market was the major market for the mini skirts marketed in 1987. The fashion industry more likely than not greatly overestimated their influence on the older, working junior market.

The point of these examples is that both youth segmentation (Phase III segmentation) and positioning on the basis of youth (Phase IV segmentation) can perhaps be hazardous for strategic marketing. One difficulty in youth segmentation is isolating the special tastes of young people and using their vernacular rather than terminology that is passe or obviously misapplied. Another is the proclivity of youth to avoid certain products or services. For instance, some librarians found that the youth segment might be an unfruitful one.

In spite of the difficulties and hazards pointed out above, there are characteristics of youth segmentation that make it rather easy to manage. It is easy to enforce price discrimination. The theory of price discrimination involves the ability to prevent the groups charged the higher price from obtaining the goods at the price given to the favored market. There are some overaged people who have gotten youth fares or youth admission to movies and entertainment facilities, just as there are some slightly underaged people who have obtained access to alcoholic beverages by stealth, but the parameters are fairly definite. The leakage occurs only at the margin. Similarly, it is relatively easy to use illustrations that create a youthful impression (young-looking models, active people).

CONSUMPTION AND YOUTH MARKETING

Our search for evidence of age-based segmentation and positioning along a youthful dimension also gives us the impression that the extent of such activity grew gradually in the 1920s and 1930s. This would be in accord with Tedlow's (1990) position that various industries adopted segmentation at different times. More importantly, if segmentation is in part a response to market conditions rather than an attempt to create those conditions, the growth of youth segmentation would be consistent with the notion that the most modern phase of consumption is a tendency to satisfy *individual* rather than *familial* needs and wants (Gordon and McArthur 1985). Obviously, people always needed clothing that was individual and consumed individual food portions. But according to Gordon and McArthur (1985), 20th century consumption has been marked by an increasing tendency to see the family as a collection of individuals with discrete desires. Youth segmentation is completely consistent with that view.

The Gordon and McArthur (1985) view, in turn, can be placed in a larger context. Fred and Grace Hechinger (1975) hold that the rise of transcendentalism in the mid-19th century led to a wholly new view of children. Instead of seeing them as innately depraved miniature adults whose evil tendencies had to be repressed (the outlook of the old fire-and-brimstone morality), the new approach saw the child as an expression of nature's beauty and innocence. This led to emphasis on protecting and developing the person's individuality. Although the transcendentalists themselves were opposed to materialism, the shift that they helped induce, placed in a materialistic society, produced the individualized buying that Gordon and McArthur (1985) describe, and thus, the material context of the "flaming youth" culture of the 1920s, the "youth market" culture of the 1960–70s, and all the intervening and subsequent youth markets.

T.J. Jackson Lears (1983) has described what he calls the "Therapeutic Ethos [of consumption]" as permeating 20th and late 19th century America. According to Lears, it stresses not only the propriety but even the *duty* of enhancing one's individual health, appearance, fitness, and capacity for the enjoyment of life. According to this interpretation, if one believes that the individual is responsible for his/her actions and life is not predestined and if one also believes that material well being and health are evidence of having led the good life, then it becomes very easy to slip over into the therapeutic view that one should take positive steps to enhance one's attributes and possessions. Since youthfulness is associated with healthfulness, it becomes a desirable quality to be implanted and inculcated by all age groups.

In many cases, advertising continues to offer self-realization and personal growth through individual health and enjoyment-of-life claims and through glimpses of intense experience associated with product consumption. Examples abound: many automobile advertisers promote the thrill of driving as a 30-second, intense experience or deliver self-realization type messages such as "you have arrived"; the well-known Calvin Klein ads of the 1980s stressed sex appeal; food advertisers ridicule what are thought to be poor eating habits (i.e., consumption of doughnuts or fatty foods for breakfast) and suggest that it is one's *duty* to eat breakfast cereals with brand names that include words like heart, health, or wise; and many exercise equipment advertisers in particular promote one's *duty* to oneself and family to stay fit.

The ascension of the beauty culture (Banner 1983) referred to in Chapter 2, and the athletic culture (Green, 1986) referred to in

Chapter 6 can be viewed as another manifestation of the therapeutic ethos. In fact, the labeling of the 1980s as the "Me Generation" may simply reflect the full blossoming of this ethos among American youth.

Lears' view is consistent with that of Gordon and McArthur (1985) and Hechinger and Hechinger (1975). As we have repeatedly noted, marketers who use the youth segmentation or youthful positioning strategy (or who use youthful looking models) usually imply health, vigor, energy, and attractiveness rather than acne, mononucleosis, or "growing pains." Consequently, the youth approach that we have examined can easily be interpreted as an expression of the therapeutic culture. In this light, the Jantzen swimsuit promotions discussed earlier are not merely an amusing and slightly risque sidelight; they are manifestations of society's and the marketers' philosophy that one *ought* to enjoy swimming, and that one *ought* to look good in a form-fitting swimsuit.

One might hypothesize that all of youth segmentation has a circular effect. To the extent that youth (and youngness) has special characteristics (or appeal), astute marketers will direct specific efforts towards those targets. These efforts could easily reinforce the sense of being desirable, which thus could lead to increased marketing. In a sense, youth could be co-opted into its suppliers' marketing strategy. It would be interesting to study whether such a process occurs with other segmentation and positioning efforts. The process could be conceived as having no limits, but clearly it does have them. Perhaps a major limitation is the attractiveness to marketers of segmenting on other bases or even of a generic (i.e., nonsegmentation or mass market) strategy (Levitt 1983).

In a way, the increased and even the specialized consumption by youth can be seen as a form of mass marketing. True, the products, services, and marketing appeals that were being aimed at youth were differentiated from those designed for younger and older groups. But whether we look at apparel or popular music or some other youth-oriented category of offerings, we see things that were intended for *masses* of youths. The specialized consumption can then be considered as a form of *mass* consumption in response to mutually reinforcing vendor and peer mass pressure. In some consumption practices, the youths may appear virtual clones. That, however, is an external view. Some particularly insightful and introspective young conformists may well recognize that they are conforming. Most, *we* suspect, see the adoption of whatever is current among their cohorts as liberalizing; as creating new opportunities, options, behaviors; as distinguishing them from other age segments; and thus, as essentially establishing their individuality.

Let us put it this way: a high school student renting a tuxedo for the senior prom may be dressing in accordance with an old, fairly standardized and continuing code; one obtaining the use of a car for cruising up and down a small town main street on Saturday night may be adhering to a more modern ritual (Orlean 1990). Neither, however, is likely to view the experience that way. Even standardized but specialized youth marketing and consumption seem to demonstrate the sort of individualism and individual hedonism that Gordon and McArthur (1985) discuss.

Segmentation versus Differentiation

This research, following upon the basis suggested by Tedlow (1990), has some implications for the concepts of market segmentation and its well-known counterpart, product differentiation. As originally presented by Wendell Smith (1956) in his famous article ''Product Differentiation and Market Segmentation as Alternative Marketing Strategies,'' the two concepts were seen as almost polar opposites, and they have typically been taught and considered as such ever since.

Product differentiation, in Smith's view, consisted of making claims that one's product was superior to competitors' in serving the desires or needs of all consumers. Differentiation may have been a relatively poor choice for the name of this concept, since it did not seem to refer to creating physical variations from the mainstream format of competitive products. Rather, it referred to inducing a belief in the general audience's mind that the product was somehow different. To cite an extreme case, a cigarette producer who advertised that its brand "was toasted" was involved in the epitome of product differentiation since: (1) toasting was a characteristic that presumably implied a more pleasant and better smoke for all consumers, even though (2) in actuality all or practically all cigarette tobacco went through a relatively similar heat drying process. Thus, the difference was purely in the mind of the beholder.

In contrast, Smith saw segmentation as adapting the product in some particular way to the desires of a specific sub-audience. A cigarette manufacturer who produced a cigarette with a red filter tip was catering solely to the female segment of the smoking market and particularly to the sub-segment that was concerned with or bothered by unsightly lipstick smears on the ends of their cigarettes.

In practice, these two concepts are not nearly as far apart as marketing theory or marketing writers have considered them. First, at the semantic level, it is clear that one item may be differentiated from its competitors by actual physical modification—as well as by adept promotional presentation. Second, as Tedlow (1990) points out, Pepsi not only recognized the existence of a demographic segment (i.e., the youthful population), but also in essence manufactured a segment of those who wanted to feel youthful. The current research indicates that many vendors feel this desire for youthfulness (even though highly idealized) is a widespead attribute of the American public. We are not by any means the first to note that segmentation may be based upon psychological rather than demographic or other external factors. The research, though, tends to point out the elusiveness of the differentiation/segmentation dichotomy as one moves away from the polar examples.

IMPLICATIONS FOR MARKETING
TO THE ELDERLY

We have already noted that emphasis on the youth market declined somewhat during the 1980s. Fewer marketing research and advertising agencies claimed to specialize in the youth market during that decade than was true in the 1960s. Strobe lighting and rock music appeared in fewer retail ambiances. The youth market remained important, both in its own right and as a guide for older consumers, and many vendors continued to emphasize appeals to the youth segment. During the 1980s, the fashionable or fad market (i.e., the one about which more was written rather than the one which engendered more new hopes among marketers) was the senior citizen or geriatric market. Authors talked of the ''greying'' rather than the ''greening'' of America. The senior market was also recognized as consisting of several sub-groups divided on one or several bases including chronological age, physical ability and debility, income status, and lifestyle. For instance, Primelife, a specialty advertising agency based in Mesa, California, divided the 50-plus grey market into six subsegments based on income, recreational preferences, and, most importantly for advertisers, television viewing and print media reading habits (Mandese 1989, p.34). As marketers turn to the senior segment, we can note several analogies and some differences from the youth market. The youth marketing experience may provide some helpful insights.

Seniors do differ from young people in many ways (some of which the seniors may themselves regret and some of which they may very well enjoy). The health problems of seniors tend to be more fundamental and obviously more life-threatening than the acne problems of teenagers. The seniors with market power are much more concerned with financial planning, capital preservation, and income maintenance than those in the youth market. They are much less of an audience for career planning advice, but more of a market for wrinkle-removal cream. Many seniors have gone through a long process of accumulating physical assets and are now in a disaccumulation phase. Some seniors are more secure in status and community relations than their younger counterparts.

Nevertheless, there are similarities between the youth and senior segments. First, obviously, both are based roughly on age, although in both cases there are some people whose demeanor, abilities, and tastes are either "young" or "old" for their chronological age.

Second, it has been said that "play is the work of children and work is the play of adults." Both the youth market and the senior market are, to a very considerable extent, outside the workforce. In this society that tends to associate merit and status with work position and success, this consumptive role can have important consequences for both groups.

Third, relatedly, both the terms "youthful" and "mature" can have negative as well as positive connotations. They both must be used with care.

Fourth, in many instances young people are searching for or setting up relationships, frequently in new settings (college, first serious job, etc.). Because of departure from occupational affiliation, death of friends and family members, and migrations to retirement communities, many seniors find themselves in much the same position. Samuel Johnson said that a man must work very hard at forming and maintaining friendships to have any in his declining years.

Fifth, both groups can harbor some suspicions of nonmembers. We all remember the slogan of the 1960s, "Do not trust anyone over 30." Many seniors are rather wary of slick young salespeople.

Some tactical suggestions for marketers flow from these analogies.

1. The terms youthful and mature, particularly the latter, must always be used in a very positive way. The senior models in advertisements, even for mobility assistance devices and the like, must always seem cheerful, active,

and vigorous. Similarly, youth advertising never por-
trays the product or service users as infantile, bedeviled,
or inadequate.

2. The importance of pricing strategy appears clear in both
   instances. We have noted that youth discounts can
   evoke a very favorable response. Few older Americans
   seem to resent being called seniors when that status is
   accompanied by a special senior price or discount. In
   fact, restaurateurs in communities with large retiree
   populations can even persuade their customers to modify
   their dining habits with, for instance, early bird discounts.

3. The desire for connectedness has motivated travel, tour,
   and retirement community promoters to place considerable emphasis on the acquisition of ''new friends'' in
   their promotional literature. There may be further opportunities for expansion of this theme.

4. Retailers need not necessarily confine their sales staff to
   the age cohorts of their customers. However, in dealing
   with both young and senior customers, the salespeople
   must be selected and trained to deal sympathetically and
   cordially with such customers. Many young people feel
   pressured and feel that they are being treated as objects
   of suspicion when served by older salespersons who do
   not radiate friendliness. Many older customers want a
   rather high degree of personal attention. They can be
   what Gregory Stone (1954) years ago called personalizing shoppers, contrasted against his economic, ethical,
   and apathetic shoppers. Personalizing shoppers derive
   satisfaction from personal interaction with sales staff.
   The older shoppers may also need help in reaching
   products, reading labels, and similar matters. Another
   way of putting it is that both youthful and mature shoppers probably tend to react very favorably to rather per-
   sonalized service. Marketers who are skilled in selling to

one group will probably find themselves deeply skilled, after some reflection, in selling the other.

ADOPTION OF YOUTH MARKETING STRATEGIES

Long before 1940, it is clear that a substantial number of marketers were directing their efforts towards a youth market or creating youth appeal for their offerings. What factors led them to adopt these strategies?

First and foremost were the ''realities'' of the marketplace. We put the term in quotation marks because the existence of a youth segment is what McCracken (1986) describes as a category into which part of the *culturally constituted* world has been parceled. We do not see culture here as being totally arbitrary; there are inherent developmental processes that make young adults different from both children and older adults. There are very basic life-cycle reasons why youth is so often the period of training, of courtship, and of family formation. But cultures can alter that pattern (e.g., delayed family formation, mid-life career retraining). Nevertheless, for the individual marketer, one of the attributes of the 19th century and subsequent American culture was increasing differentiation of and increasing attention to youth.

Little imagination was needed to perceive that the primary market for maternity dresses and pre-prepared baby foods consisted of women of childbearing age. The contribution was in conceiving products that met the special needs of that special group. In other instances, such as the case of ordinary male and female clothing, considerable acumen was required to understand that youths' tastes differed from the preferences of their seniors. That the tastes of those seniors frequently included a desire to assume the physical appearance of youthfulness has also been a well-established "reality" of the American marketplace. The response to those realities is evidence that many pre-1940 marketers had the sensitivity and innovativeness of their more recent counterparts even though they lacked some current technological skills.

Second, marketing and particularly consumer goods and services marketing is very public. By their very nature, promotional campaigns, product offerings, price policies, and distribution practices are exposed to competitors as well as to customers. In the Darwinian market world, the successful survivors (the terms are redundant) tend to have developed very sensitive antennae with which to judge rival performance. Thus, successful youth segmentation or youth targeting by one entrepreneur quickly becomes a consideration in others' strategy formulations.

Third, as we have noted, some (perhaps many) media with youthful audiences had a vested interest in encouraging youth marketing. Their space salespeople must have steadily urged attention to the youth market.

Finally, entrepreneurs, consultants, and marketing scholars expounded the significance of the youth market. The willingness to share advice and information has often been a startling characteristic of American enterprise. An enormous volume of information flows through trade and professional conventions and journals. There is chaff along with the wheat, but the trained ear knows what to listen for. The United States has been a land of consultants ever since the days of Frederick Taylor and the efficiency experts. They serve as arbitrageurs of information in addition to exercising their own creative and technical skills.

There have been many forces to push and to pull marketers toward youth segmentation. Why did more not use it even sooner? The answer, of course, is again in part in the reality that market segmentation can be based on many criteria. Some marketers have little need for segmentation: Resnik, Turney, and Mason (1979) called the aggregation of segments countersegmentation. In some instances, the first youth segmenter in a category may have preempted the strategy. Could, and would and should, Coca–Cola advertise "We are even Younger"? In addition, some marketers, such as Robert Kahn's clothing store employer, are simply slower on their feet than their rivals. The important thing is that many did use youth segmentation.

An important point concerns the apparent apex in youth marketing during the late 1960s and early 1970s when the great Baby Boom youth population peaked. Gilbert (1957) and *Printers' Ink* (1961) predicted, on the basis of insurance and census data, that youth marketing would grow substantially with the relative visibility of youth. In the previous paragraphs, we argued that youth marketing is in part a function of American cultural development. But here we have evidence of youth marketing as being a function of youths' relative size in the population. It is, in fact, currently a function of both. Once the cultural foundations had been laid for youth marketing in the late 19th and early 20th century, later marketers were able to easily predict increases in youth market opportunities based on population trends. Indeed, if youth marketing had not already existed, they probably ultimately would have created it. The number of youth grew from 22.3 million in 1950 (14.7 percent of the U.S. population) to 36.5 million in 1970 (17.8 percent). As it declines to a predicted 36.1 million in the year 2000 (13.5 percent) (Engel, Blackwell, and Miniard 1986), one of the lowest proportions in the history of the United States, marketers' and writers' attention will undoubtedly shift, especially if youth becomes less vocal.

George Fisk (1988) has provided an interesting classification for marketing history. He sees marketing change as being either evolutionary or revolutionary, and either random or determinant. These categories are useful, even though they ultimately depend on perspective and depth of analysis.

Economic historians argue whether there was an Industrial Revolution or an Industrial Evolution. The choice of terminology depends on how great the changes seem in relation to how long the time span appears. Placing youth segmentation within the scope of marketing history, we opt for "evolutionary." Certainly mar-

keting segmentation, at its technical best, is far more complex and
sophisticated than it was in 1890, 1920, or even 1940. Moreover,
the extent of its utilization has undoubtedly increased. As Braden
and Endelman (1990) point out, travel segmentation on all bases
(age, gender, power, interest, health, etc.) has been an increasingly
important aspect of the tourist industry throughout the 20th century. But the word "increasingly" is key. The study demonstrates
that youth segmentation and positioning were used in the 19th
century and enjoyed much growth in the first four decades of this
century. That growth could also be considered predictable or determinant *if* one could predict:

1. Demographics
2. The economic and technical changes that lead to increased education and prolonged dependency
3. The continued growth of individualism
4. The continued cultural valuation of youthfulness
5. The long-term striving of marketers for differential advantage

The motivation of marketers and the strength of their managerial drive was certainly predictable by the end of the 19th century.
Their future choices of technologies were undoubtedly less clear.
America's fascination with youth and youthfulness was apparent.
The movement toward individualism, the culture of consumption,
and the therapeutic culture were all under way as a result of even
earlier philosophic foundations. America was becoming more industrial, urban, and technological. These tendencies became even
more marked as the nation moved into the early decades of the
20th century. Thus, retrospectively, we can isolate much of the
systematic forces that fueled the evolution of youth marketing. In
that sense, the pattern was really quite determinant.

Yet we cannot conclude that we have constructed an ironclad
chain of cause and effect that should have been clear to our earliest
predecessors in the teaching of marketing and applied economics.

How much of the present state of youth marketing is due to the fact that things that could have happened did not occur? For example, what would youth marketing be like in America today if the Great Depression of the 1930s had been even more severe and had resulted in revolution? What if we had lost World War II? What if a different rate of development in medical/public health technologies had led to a different population age mix than that which actually occurred? We cannot answer these or many other similar questions; thankfully, we don't have to answer them. It has been said that the historian's motto is: "The future is certain, only the past is subject to debate." Certainty, however, is not tantamount to foreseeability.

CONCLUSION

For many older consumers, the Ponce de Leon Fountain of Youth appeal of youngness remains. George Bernard Shaw said that "youth is wasted on the young." This book indicates that marketers have long felt that it was not wasteful to concentrate on youth.

The answer to the question "Was there a Pepsi Generation before Pepsi discovered it?" is *yes*. This does not detract from Pepsi's clever tapping of the youth theme at an appropriate time.

R E F E R E N C E S

Abrams, Mark (1948), "The British Cinema Audience," *Hollywood Quarterly,* 3 (Winter), 155-8.

Adler, Marilyn (1987), "Student Buying Rates High Interest," *Advertising Age,* 58 (February 2), 1.

Advertising Age (1988), *Proctor & Gamble: The House that Ivory Built,* Lincolnwood, IL: NTC Business Press.

Alexander, Carter and W. W. Theisen (1920), "Campaigns for Teachers' Salaries," *Educational Review,* 60 (October), 190-204.

———— (1921), *Publicity Campaigns for Better School Support,* New York: World Book Company.

Alexander, Suzanne (1990), "Marketers Find College Crowd a Tough Test," *The Wall Street Journal,* (April 16), B1+.

Allen, Robert C. and Douglas Gomery (1985), *Film History: Theory and Practice,* New York: McGraw-Hill.

Allen, Robert F. (1933), "Talking to 6,000,000 Rulers," *Printers' Ink,* (October 26), 12-3+.

Bailey, Beth L. (1988), *From Front Porch to Back Seat: Courtship in Twentieth Century America,* Baltimore: The John Hopkins University Press.

Baird, D. G. (1931), "All States Life Opens a Big Market Among College Alumni," *Sales Management,* 25 (February 28), 372-3+.

Baker, Henry G. (1953), *Rich's of Atlanta,* Atlanta Division, University of Georgia.

Ballard, Helen A. (1919), "The Child Appeal as a Factor in Merchandising a Product," *Printers' Ink,* 107 (June 19), 93–6.

Banner, Lois (1983), *American Beauty,* New York: Alfred A. Knopf.

Barker, B. Brown (1930), "A Choice Bit of College Publicity," *Association of American Colleges Bulletin,* 26 (December), 489–90.

Bernays, Edward L. (1965), *Biography of An Idea: Memoirs of Public Relations Counsel Edward L. Bernays,* New York: Simon and Schuster.

Bliven, Bruce J. (1954), *The Wonderful Typing Machine,* New York: Random House.

Boorstin, Daniel J. (1973), *The Americans: The Democratic Experience,* New York: Vintage Books.

Bradbury, Amos (1933), "Advertising to Seven Million Young Skeptics," *Printers' Ink,* 162 (February 2), 17–20.

Braden, Donna R. and Judith E. Endelman (1990), *America on Vacation,* Dearborn, MI: Henry Ford Museum and Greenfield Village.

Bryant, Joyce E. (1990), Vice President, Consumer Affairs of Household International, letter to Stanley C. Hollander, Nov. 3.

Bulletin of the National Retail Dry Goods Association (1938a), "What Constitutes the Market for Father's Day Merchandise?" 20 (May), 22–3.

———— (1938b), "How Morgan & Co. Put Montreal on Skis—Their Skis," 20 (May), 18–20.

———— (1938c), "Winter Sports Plans," 20 (September), 31–2+.

———— (1939), "Organization of A Women's Dress Department: The Large Miss," 21 (May), 22.

Burns, Pete E. F. (1926) "Selling the College Market," *Printers' Ink,* 137 (October 7), 49–50+.

Carmical, Andrew L. (1928), "To Sell Today—Appeal to Youth," *Sales Management,* 15 (September 15), 645+.

Case, Francis H. (1921), *Handbook of Church Advertising,* New York: The Abingdon Press.

Chatauqua Institution (1938), *When Planning Your Vacation, Decide on Chatauqua,* New York: Chatauqua Institution brochure.

Cherington, Paul T. (1924), "Statistics in Market Studies," *The Annals of the American Academy of Political and Social Science,* 115 (September), 130–5.

Clark, John Bates (1924), *The Economics of Overhead Costs,* Chicago: University of Chicago Press. Reported in Backman, Jules (1953), *Price Practices and Price Policies,* New York: The Ronald Press.

Cobb, Margaret V. (1921), "How College Girls Buy," *Printers' Ink,* 116 (August 25), 111–2.

College Humor (1928), *An Approach to the College Market,* New York: College Humor.

Collegiate Special Advertising, Inc. (1928), *The Local Ad Handbook,* New York: Collegiate Special Advertising Agency, Inc.

Conant, Jennet and Pat Wingert (1987), "Hold on to Those Hems," *Newsweek,* (April 27), 69–70.

Coutant, Frank R. and Everett R. Smith (1938), "Your Customers' Ages and Incomes," *Advertising and Selling,* 38 (September), 29–32+.

Crosby, Lawrence A., James D. Gill and Robert E. Lee (1984), "Life Status and Age in Predictors of Value Orientation," in *Personal Values and Consumer Psychology,* Robert E. Pitts and Arch G. Woodside, eds., Lexington, MA: D. C. Heath, 201–18.

Cutlip, Scott M. (1965), *Fund Raising in the United States,* New Brunswick, NJ: Rutgers.

———— (1970), "Advertising Higher Education: The Early Years of College Public Relations," *College and University Journal,* 9 (Fall), 21–8.

———— (1971), "Advertising and Education: The Early Years of College Public Relations—Part II," *College and University Journal,* 10 (January), 25–33.

Day, Rebecca (1989), "Koss Goes to College," *Adweek,* 30 (August 21), 28.

DeCamp, Oscar (1929), "Winning the Younger Market Without Losing the Old," *Printers' Ink,* 146 (January 21), 101–2.

Dickinson, Roy (1919), "Army Makes Drastic Change in Advertising Appeal," *Printers' Ink,* 107 (May 1), 65–8.

———— (1932), "162,000 Inquiries in Three Months by this Company," *Printers' Ink,* 158 (January 7), 73–5.

Donnell, Rena R. (1940), "Customer Advisory Committees in Retail Stores," *Journal of Retailing,* 16 (October), 71–5.

Donovan, W. J. (1938), "Winter Sports: What Are This Season's Prospects?," *Bulletin of the National Retail Dry Goods Association,* 20 (September), 29.

Dumont, Harry (1929), " 'Spangles' Strikes Pay Dirt in the College Market," *Sales Management,* 18 (April 6), 18–9.

Duncan, B. J. (1923), "Capturing the Home Citadel through the Nursery," *Printers' Ink Monthly,* 25 (October), 36+.

Eddy, Sherwood (1944), *A Century With Youth: A History of the Y.M.C.A. from 1844 to 1944,* New York: Association Press.

Edwin Alden & Bro's American Newspaper Catalogue (1882), Cincinnati, OH.

Elliot, Frank R. (1932), "Publicity and Education," *Journal of Higher Education*, 3 (June), 303-8.

Elliott, Eugene Ernest (1920), *How to Advertise a Church*, New York: George H. Doran Company.

Ellison, C. L. (1934), "Free Billiard Lessons," *Printers' Ink*, 169 (November 22), 25-7.

Elsworth, R. H. (1899), "How the University of Michigan is Advertised," *Printers' Ink*, 27 (May 31), 3-4.

Emmett, Elizabeth (1926), "Alice in Beautyland," *Printers' Ink*, 136 (September 9), 105-6+.

Engel, James F., Roger D. Blackwell and Paul W. Miniard (1986), *Consumer Behavior*, New York: The Dryden Press.

Erbes, P. H. (1937), "The Campus Looks at Advertising," *Printers' Ink Monthly*, 34 (March), 58+.

Ewen, David (1977), *All the Years of American Popular Music*, Englewood Cliffs, NJ: Prentice-Hall.

Fannis, Rebecca (1984), "Marketing to Teens: All Talk and No Action," *Marketing and Media Decisions*, 19 (July), 42-3+.

Fallows, Alice K. (1901), "Working One's Way through College," *The Century Magazine*, 62 (2), 163-77.

Fass, Paula S. (1977), *The Damned and the Beautiful: American Youth in the 1920s*, New York: Oxford University Press.

Fisk, George (1988), "Interactive System Frameworks for Analyzing SpaceTime Changes in Marketing Structures and Processes," in *Historical Perspectives in Marketing: Essays in Honor of Stanley C. Hollander*, Terrence Nevett and Ronald A. Fullerton, eds., Lexington, KY: Lexington Books, 55-70.

Forkner, Hamden L. and Ron C. DeYoung (1976), "A Historical Development of Shorthand," in *Business Education Yesterday, Today and Tomorrow (National Business Education Yearbook, No. 14)*, Ruth B. Woolschlager and E. Edward Harris, eds., Reston, VA: National Business Education Association.

Fox, Vivian (1977), "Is Adolescence a Phenomenon of Modern Times?" *Journal of Psychohistory*, 5 (Fall), 271-90.

Fratis, Sue L. and Elizabeth Arlett (1920), "Two Successful School Campaigns," *Teachers College Record*, 21 (January), 68-75.

Frederick, Christine (1924), "New Wealth, New Standards of Living and Changed Family Budgets," *The Annals of the American Academy of Political and Social Science*, 115 (September), 74-82.

_____ (1929), *Selling Mrs. Consumer,* New York: The Business Course.

Frederick, Lewis Allen (1931), *Only Yesterday: An Informal History of the Nineteen-Twenties,* New York: Harper.

Fullerton, Ronald A. (1985), "Segmentation Strategies and Practices in the 19th Century German Book Trade: A Case Study in the Development of a Major Marketing Technique," in *Historical Perspectives in Consumer Research: National and International Perspectives,* Chin T. Tand and Jagdish N. Sheth, eds., Singapore: National University of Singapore, 135-9.

_____ (1988), "How Modern is Modern Marketing? Marketing's Evolution and the Myth of the 'Production Era,' " *Journal of Marketing,* 52 (January), 108-25.

_____ (1990), "The Art of Marketing Research: Selections from Paul F. Lazarfield's 'Shoe Buying in Zurich,' " *Journal of the Academy of Marketing Science,* 18 (Fall), 319-27.

Gage, Theodore J. (1982), "Prospecting in the Off-Campus Gold Mine," *Advertising Age,* 53 (August 2), 18-20.

Gelman, David (1990), "A Much More Riskier Passage," *Newsweek: Special Edition,* (Summer/Fall), 10+.

George, Lloyd (1929), "The College Market for Aircraft," *Airway Age,* 10 (May), 670-2.

Gilbert, Eugene (1957), *Advertising and Marketing to Young People,* Pleasantville, NY: Printers' Ink Books.

Giles, Ray (1922), "Making Youth the Bull's-Eye of the Advertising Target," *Printers' Ink,* 120 (September 14), 57-8+.

Gillespie, Karen (1990), personal conversation with former director of the New York University Institute of Retail Management.

Gillis, John R. (1974), *Youth and History,* New York: Academic Press.

Goldblatt, Ellen (1990), personal conversation with director of research at Muzak.

Gomery, Douglas (1990), "The Movie Palace Comes to America's Cities," in *For Fun and Profit: The Transformation of Leisure into Consumption,* Richard Butsch, ed., Philadelphia: Temple University Press, 136-51.

Gordon, Jean and Jan McArthur (1985), "American Women and Domestic Consumption 1800-1920: Four Interpretive Themes," *Journal of American Culture,* 8 (Fall), 35-46.

Goss, E. Lyle (1988), Personal correspondence with past president of National Association of College Stores.

Graebner, William (1987), "Outlawing Teenage Populism: The Campaign Against Secret Societies in the American High School: 1900–1950," *Journal of American History,* 74 (December), 411–36.

———— (1990), *Coming of Age in Buffalo: Youth and Authority in the Postwar Era,* Philadelphia: Temple University Press.

Gras, N.S.B. (1942), *Harvard Co-operative Society Past and Present 1882–1942,* Cambridge, MA: Harvard University Press.

———— and Henrietta M. Larson (1939), *Casebook in American Business History,* New York: F. S. Crofts & Co.

Gray, William S. and Ruth Monroe (1929), *The Reading Interests and Habits of Adults,* New York: Macmillan.

Green, Harvey (1986), *Fit For America: Health, Fitness, Sport and American Society,* New York: Parthenon Books.

Gridley, Don (1923), "Ideas That Are Making Sales to and through Children," *Printers' Ink Monthly,* 7 (November), 31–2.

Griffith, Frederick, Jr. (1982), *Men Wanted for the U.S. Army: America's Experience with an All-Volunteer Army between the World Wars,* Westport, CT: Greenwood Press.

Grumbine, E. Evalyn (1934), "This Juvenile Market," *Printers' Ink,* 168 (July 19), 12+.

Hall, Jacquelyn Dowd, James Leloudis, Robert Korstad, Mary Murphy, Lu Anne Jones and Christopher B. Daley (1987), *Like A Family: The Making of a Southern Mill Town,* Chapel Hill, NC: The University of North Carolina Press.

Hamm, Charles (1979), *Yesterday: Popular Song in America,* New York: W. S. Norton.

Handel, Leo A. (1950), *Hollywood Looks at its Audience: A Report of Film Audience Research,* Urbana, IL: The University of Illinois Press.

Hanson, Joseph H. (1940), "How About Starting A Soldiers' Supply Department," *Bulletin of the National Retail Dry Goods Association,* 22 (October), 16.

Hardy, Stephen (1990), "'Adopted by All the Leading Clubs': Sporting Goods and the Shaping of Leisure, 1800–1900," in *For Fun and Profit: The Transformation of Leisure into Consumption,* Richard Butsch, ed., Philadelphia: Temple University Press, 71–103.

Harrod, Frederick S. (1978), *Manning the New Navy: The Development of a Modern Naval Enlisted Force, 1899–1940,* Westport, CT: Greenwood Press.

Hart, Joseph K. (1925), "The Automobile in the Middle Ages," *Survey,* 54 (August 1), 493–7.

Hauser, Grady (1986), ''How Teenagers Spend the Family Dollar,'' *American Demographics,* 8 (December), 38–41.

Hawes, Joseph M. and N. Ray Hines (1985), *American Childhood: A Research Guide and Historical Handbook,* Westport, CT: Greenwood Press.

Hechinger, Fred M. and Grace Hechinger (1975), *Growing Up in America,* New York: McGraw–Hill.

Helitzer, Melvin and Carl Heyel (1970), *The Youth Market: Its Dimensions, Influence and Opportunities for You,* New York: Media Books.

Historical Statistics of the United States, Colonial Times to 1970: Bicentennial Issues, Part 1 (1975), Washington, D.C.: Government Printing Office.

Holbrook, Morris B. and Robert M. Schindler (1989), ''Some Exploratory Findings on the Development of Musical Tastes,'' *Journal of Consumer Research,* 16 (June), 119–24.

Hollander, Stanley (1984), ''Herbert Hoover, Professor Levitt, Simplification and the Marketing Concept,'' in *Scientific Method in Marketing,* Paul Anderson and Michael Ryan, eds., Chicago: American Marketing Association, 260–3.

———— (1986), ''The Marketing Concept—A Deja View,'' in *Marketing: Management Technology as a Social Process,* George Fisk, ed., New York: Praeger Publishers, 3–29.

Hopkins, C. Howard (1951), *History of the Y.M.C.A. in North America,* New York: The Association Press.

Howe, Andrew M. (1931), ''25,000 Inquiries in Ten Days,'' *Printers' Ink,* 155 (April 16), 49–50+.

Hower, Ralph Merle (1949), *The History of an Advertising Agency,* Cambridge, MA: Harvard University Press.

Hudson, Ray M. (1928), ''Organized Effort in Simplification,'' *The Annals of the American Academy of Political and Social Science,* 137 (May), 1–8.

Hulin-Salkin, Belinda (1982), ''Media Cool—But Not to College Crowd,'' *Advertising Age,* 53 (August 2), 7+.

Hyers, Faith Holmes (1927), ''The Library and the Advertising World,'' *Library Journal,* 52 (June 1), 575–6.

Irwin, Alfreda L. (1990), Correspondence with historian-in-residence, Chatauqua Historical Society.

Jacobson, Sol (1928), ''Successful Merchandising of a Boy's Clothing Department,'' *Journal of Retailing,* 3 (January), 7–11.

Johnson, Owen (1912), *Stover at Yale,* New York: Crossett & Dunlap.

Johnson, Wendall F. (1920), ''Selling the Library to Professional Men,''
    Library Journal, 45 (March 1), 207-8.
Journal of Retailing (1928), ''Sectionalizing Apparel Departments,'' 3 (January), 13.
Kahn, Robert (1988), *Retailing Today,* LaFayette, CA: Robert Kahn and
    Associates Newsletter (August 23).
Keeler, Floyd Y. (1919), ''The Background of the Recent Army Advertising Campaign,'' *Printers' Ink,* 108 (August 28), 121-2+.
Konrad, Walecia (1990), ''Book Review,'' *Business Week,* 3156 (April
    23), 14-5.
Kotler, Philip (1980), *Principles of Marketing,* Englewood Cliffs, NJ: Prentice-Hall.
Kuenstler, Walter P. (1940), ''The Buying Habits of Women Students
    on the University of Pennsylvania Campus,'' *Journal of Marketing,* 5
    (October), 166-7.
Larned, W. Livingston (1927), ''Youth Rides Triumphant in Modern
    Advertising,'' *Printers' Ink,* 140 (September 1), 145-6+.
Lazarfield, Paul F. (1947), ''Audience Research in the Movie Field,''
    The Annuals of the American Academy of Political and Social Science, 254
    (November), 160-8.
Lears, T. J. Jackson (1983), ''From Salvation to Self-Realization: Advertising and the Therapeutic Roots of the Consumer Culture,'' in *The
    Culture of Consumption: Critical Essays in American History, 1880-1980,*
    Richard W. Fox and T. J. Jackson Lears, eds., New York: Pantheon
    Books.
Lehman-Haupt, Christopher (1990), ''Review of *The Final Club* by Geoffrey Wolff,'' *The New York Times* (Midwestern Edition), September
    10, B2.
Lencek, Lena and Gideon Bosker (1989), *Making Waves: Swimsuits and the
    Undressing of America,* San Francisco, CA: Chronicle Books.
Levitt, Theodore (1983), ''The Globalization of Markets,'' *Harvard Business Review,* 61 (May-June), 92-102.
Lewis, Howard T. (1933), *The Motion Picture Industry,* New York: D. van
    Norstrand.
Lewis, Orlando P. (1904), ''The Self-Supporting Student in American
    Colleges,'' *North American Review,* 179 (November), 718-30.
Link, Henry C. and Harry Arthur Hopf (1946), *People and Books* New
    York: Book Manufacturers' Institute.
Literary Digest (1926), ''A Jazz Appeal to 'Flaming Youth,' '' 89 (April
    24), 28.

Lloyd, Alan C. (1990), veteran typing and business education teacher, textbook writer, and former official of the Business Education Association, letter to Stanley C. Hollander, Nov. 6.

Loudon, David L. and Albert J. Della Bitta (1984), *Consumer Behavior: Concepts and Applications,* New York: McGraw-Hill.

Love, John F. (1986), *McDonald's: Behind the Arches,* New York: Bantam Books.

Lyons, Emanual (1933), *2,222 Retailing Ideas,* Pittstown, NJ: The Author.

Maltby, Richard (1989), *Dreams for Sale,* London: Harrup (An American version was also published in 1989 as *The Passing Parade: A Cultural History of the United States,* New York: Oxford Press).

Mandese, Joe (1989), "The New Old," *Marketing and Media Decisions,* 4 (April), 32-4+.

Marchand, Roland (1985), *Advertising the American Dream: Making Way for Modernity, 1920-1940,* Berkeley, CA: University of California Press.

Marts, A. C. (1932), "The Colleges in Newspapers," *Association of American College Bulletin,* 18 (May), 246-9.

Mathes, James M. (1933), "Tough Times, Young Man, But Listen Here!" *Printers' Ink,* 165 (November 16), 17-8+.

McCracken, Grant (1986), "Culture and Consumption: A Theoretical Account of the Structure and Movement of the Cultural Meaning of Consumer Goods," *Journal of Consumer Research,* 13 (June), 71-84.

McCullough, E. W. (1928), "The Relation of the Chamber of Commerce of the United States of America to the Growth of the Simplifications Program in American Industry," *The Annals of the American Academy of Political and Social Science,* 137 (May), 9-16.

McDonough, G. B. (1938), "Activities of the San Francisco Branch of the Sewing Institute," *Bulletin of the National Retail Dry Goods Association,* 20 (March), 116-7.

McJohnston, Harrison (1916), "How One Leading University is Advertising," *Printers' Ink,* 96 (August 31), 85-6+.

McKendrick, Neil, John Brewer and J. H. Plumb (1982), *The Birth of a Consumer Society: The Commercialization of Eighteenth-Century England,* London: Europa Publications Limited.

McNair, Malcolm P. and Charles I. Gragg (1930), *Problems in Retail Distribution,* New York: McGraw-Hill.

Mihaly, George (1984), "Youth Must be Served," *Madison Avenue,* 18 (November), 48+.

Moschis, George P. (1987), *Consumer Socialization: A Life-Style Perspective,* Lexington, KY: Lexington Books.

Muller, Charles (1931), "Don't Overlook the Sons and Daughters of Mr. and Mrs. Consumer," *Printers' Ink*, 155 (May 21), 57–8+.

National Retail Dry Goods Association Controllers' Congress (1934), *1933 Departmental Merchandising and Operating Results for Department Stores and Specialty Stores*, New York: National Retail Dry Goods Association.

Nemetz, Carl J. (1939), "How to Operate a Cooperative Store within a High School," *Journal of Retailing*, 15 (October), 89–92.

The New York Times (1987), "Short Skirts: Big Sales," (September 29), A32.

Nichols, G. A. (1919), "Athletic Goods Manufacturers to Popularize Outdoor Sports," *Printers' Ink*, 107 (May 29), 25–7.

North, H. C. (1929), "Sell the College Market—It Is Wide Open," *Sales Management*, 17 (January 5), 24–5.

N. W. Ayer & Son's American Newspaper Annual (1882), Philadelphia.

Nystrom, Paul H. (1928), *Economics of Fashion*, New York: The Ronald Press Company.

——— (1929), *Economic Principles of Consumption*, New York: The Ronald Press Company.

Orlean, Susan (1990), *Saturday Night*, New York: Alfred A. Knopf.

Palmer, Dewey H. and Frederick J. Schlink (1934), "Education and the Consumer," *The Annals of the American Academy of Political and Social Science*, 173 (May), 188–96.

Paoletiff, Jo B. and Carol L. Krelogh (1989), "The Children's Department," in *Men and Women: Dressing the Part*, Claudia Brush Kidwell and Valerie Steele, eds., Washington: Smithsonian Institution Press.

Park, Robert J. (1989), "Healthy, Moral and Strong: Educational Views of Exercise and Athletics in 19th Century America," in *Fitness in American Culture: Images of Health, Sport, and the Body, 1830–1940*, Kathryn Grover, ed., Amherst, MA and Rochester, NY: University of Massachusetts Press and The Margaret Wodbury Strong Museum, 123–68.

Peel, Mark (1986), "On the Margins: Lodgers and Boarders in Boston, 1860–1900," *Journal of American History*, 72 (March), 813–34.

Peiss, Kathy (1990), "Commercial Leisure and the 'Women Question,' " in *For Fun and Profit: The Transformation of Leisure into Consumption*, Richard Butsch, ed., Philadelphia: Temple University Press, 105–17.

Peterson, Ruth C. and L. L. Thurstone (1933), "Motion Pictures and the Social Attitudes of Children," in *Motion Pictures and Youth*, W. W. Charters, ed., New York: Macmillan.

Peterson, Theodore (1964), *Magazines in the Twentieth Century,* Urbana, IL: University of Illinois Press.

Pence, Owen E. and William E. Speers (1946), *The Y.M.C.A. and Social Need: A Study of Institutional Adaptation,* New York: The Association Press.

Photoplay Magazine (1922), *The Age Factor in Selling and Advertising,* New York: *Photoplay Magazine.*

Poffenberger, Albert T. (1925), *Psychology in Advertising,* New York: A. W. Shaw Company.

Pollay, Richard W. (1985), "The Subsiding Sizzle: A Descriptive History of Print Advertising, 1900–1980," *Journal of Marketing,* 49 (Summer), 24–37.

———. (1983), "The Subsiding Sizzle: Shifting Strategies in Twentieth Century Magazine Advertising," in *First American Workshop in Marketing History: Proceedings of a Conference Held at Michigan State University,* Stanley C. Hollander and Ronald Savitt, eds., East Lansing: Michigan State University Department of Marketing and Transportation Administration, 102–17.

Potter, David Morris (1954), *People of Plenty,* Chicago: University of Chicago Press.

Printers' Ink (1896), "Young Men in Season," 16 (August 5), 8.

——— (1904a), "Weekly Ad Contest," 46 (March 23), 42–3.

——— (1904b), "School Advertising," 47 (April 27), 44.

——— (1904c), "Advertising a University," 48 (September 21), 10-1.

——— (1905a), "Commercial Art Criticism," 51 (May 3), 52.

——— (1905b), "Advertising a Private School," 52 (July 19), 18-9.

——— (1905c), "A Voting Contest for Scholarships," 53 (November 8), 34.

——— (1915a), "College Students Write Ads for 'Fatima,'" 90 (March 11), 25-6.

——— (1915b), "Victor's Methods of Developing Sales to Public Schools," 91 (April 22), 17-9.

——— (1915c), "Campaigning on Future Big Buyers While They Are Students," 93 (December 30), 10-3+.

——— (1916), "Getting at Future Big Buyer in School," 94 (March 16), 71-2.

——— (1917a), "U.S. Marine Corps Advertising for Recruits," 98 (January 4), 73-4+.

——— (1917b), "Universities to Make Up Student Losses through Advertising," 100 (August 2), 25-6.

_____ (1919a), "Army Officers Get Advertising Instruction," 106 (March 6), 86.

_____ (1919b), "Major Sterrett, U.S. Marine, Enters Advertising," 107 (May 1), 57–8.

_____ (1919c), "Selling the Sea to the Mississippi Valley," 107 (June 5), 77–8.

_____ (1919d), "U.S. Army Will Use Paid Advertising," 107 (June 5), 91–2.

_____ (1919e), "The U.S. Army a University in Khaki, Campaign Keynote," 107 (June 12), 45–7.

_____ (1919f), "Navy to Spend $250,000 in Advertising for Recruits," 108 (July 17), 19–20.

_____ (1919g), "The Coming Navy Recruiting Campaign," 108 (September 11), 32–3.

_____ (1919h), "Navy Poster Advertisement Reproduced in Real Life," 109 (December 11), 117.

_____ (1919i), "Switzerland Advertises Itself in America," 109 (December 11), 153–4+.

_____ (1919j), "Army to Use Newspapers for Recruiting," 109 (December 25), 32.

_____ (1920a), "Army Starts Its Intensive Campaign," 110 (January 29), 19–20.

_____ (1920b), "Cornell University Uses Paid Space," 110 (February 19), 35–6.

_____ (1920c), "Colleges Unite in Advertising to 'Prospects,'" 112 (September 2), 105–6+.

_____ (1920d), "Study Pure Science, Urges General Electric," 113 (November 25), 125–6+.

_____ (1922), "Fitting Your Copy to the Medium," 120 (September 7), 8+.

_____ (1923a), "Advertising Aids in Eight-Year Endowment Campaign," 122 (January 11), 89–90.

_____ (1923b), "How the University of Maine Advertises to Reach Alumni," 122 (February 1), 127–8.

_____ (1924), "A Bank Offers College Scholarship In Essay Contest," 126 (February 24), 124.

_____ (1926), "Iowa Agricultural College Uses Advertisers' Booklets," 134 (January 21), 73–4.

_____ (1927), "A Public Library Advertises for Customers," 139 (June 30), 116.

_____ (1931), "What Kinds of Advertising Material Will Schools Use?" 154 (January 8), 121+.

_____ (1933), "30 Million Young, Eager Prospects for Advertisers," 162 (February 16), 16.

_____ (1935), "Cups on Campus," 170 (January 3), 41.

_____ (1936), "Educating Youth," 177 (November 15), 64+.

_____ (1937), "Help from the Colleges," 178 (March 11), 84-5+.

_____ (1961), "Postwar Expansion in Size and Value Presages What Is to Come," 276 (September 1), 56-7.

Printers' Ink Monthly (1938), "For Educational Purposes," 26 (February), 17-9+.

Pritchett, Thomas K. and Betty M. Pritchett (1990), "The Marketing of Religion: 1900-1930," in *Essays in Economic and Business History: Volume VIII,* Edwin J. Perkins, ed., Los Angeles: University of Southern California, 147-57.

Quiett, Glenn C. and Ralph D. Casey (1926), *Principles of Publicity,* New York: D. Appleton and Company.

Railsback, H. R. (1945), correspondence from the director of advertising, Deere & Company, to a distributor.

Resnik, Alan J., Peter B. B. Turney and J. Barry Mason (1979), "Marketers Turn to 'Countersegmentation,'" *Harvard Business Review,* 57 (September-October), 100-6.

Rich, Kimberly A. (1991), curator, Hallmark Historical Collection, Hallmark Cards, letter to Stanley C. Hollander, April 3.

Richards, Florence (1951), *The Ready-to-Wear Industry: 1900-1950,* New York: Fairchild Publications.

Robinson, D. E. (1924), "Advertising for Students at a Profit," *Printers' Ink,* 128 (July 24), 160-1.

Roehl, Craig H. (1989), *The Piano in America: 1890-1940,* Chapel Hill: University of North Carolina Press.

Russell, Frederick A. (1926), "The Changing College Market," *Sales Management,* 11 (December 25), 1071-2+.

Rudelius, William and John R. Walton (1987), "Improving the Managerial Relevance of Market Segmentation Studies," in *Review of Marketing: 1987,* Michael J. Houston, ed., Chicago: American Marketing Association, 385-404.

Sales Management (1933), "How College Students Spend: $300 Annually at Berea; $2,000 at Bryn-Mawr," 32 (January 15), 87.

_____ (1934), "What the College Market Is Buying and Will Buy," 35 (November 15), 506-7+.

_____ (1936), "Growing Army of Young Skeptics Imperils Success of Sales Drive," 38 (January 15), 80–1+.

Sanjek, Russell (1988), *American Popular Music and its Business: The First Four Hundred Years: Volume III. From 1900–1984,* New York: Oxford University Press.

Scherer, Miriam (1941), "Fashion Forecasting," *Journal of Retailing,* 17 (October), 69–77.

Schacter, Henry W. (1930), *Profitable Department Store Management,* New York: Harper.

Schmidt, Alvin J. (1980), *Fraternal Organizations,* Westport, CT: Greenwood Press.

Shannon, Monica (1921), "Los Angeles' Library Campaign," *Library Journal,* 46 (September 1), 703–4.

Shaw, Arch W. (1916), *An Approach to Business Problems,* Cambridge, MA: Harvard University Press.

Shepard, George (1935), "Advertising for Future Markets," *Advertising and Selling,* 26 (November 7), 32–3.

Sherman, Sidney A. (1900), "Advertising in the United States," *Journal of the American Statistical Association,* New Series No. 52 (December), p. 119–161.

Sheth, Jagdish N. (1991), keynote speech, *Fifth Conference on Historical Research on Marketing and Marketing Thought,* Michigan State University, East Lansing, April 19, 1991.

Shuttleworth, Frank K. and Mark A. May (1933), "The Social Conduct and Attitudes of Movie Fans," in *Motion Pictures and Youth,* W. W. Charters, ed., New York: Macmillan.

Sinruer, H. R. (1990), archival consultant to B'nai B'rith, letter to Stanley C. Hollander, June 19.

Sinsheimer, Allen (1926), *Retail Advertising of Men's and Boy's Wear,* New York: Harper.

Sloan, Pat and Judith Graham (1988), "Skirting Matters for Fall: What Goes Up, Comes Down," *Advertising Age,* (April 11), 32.

Smith, Herbert Heebner (1915), *Publicity and Progress,* New York: George H. Doran Company.

Smith, Jane Webb (1990), *Smoke Signals* (catalogue of an exhibit at the Valentine Museum, Richmond VA, April–October), Richmond, VA: Valentine Museum, distributed by University of North Carolina Press, Chapel Hill, NC.

Smith, Wendell R. (1956), "Product Differentiation and Market Segmentation as Alternative Marketing Strategies," *Journal of Marketing,* 21 (July), 3–8.

Sorenson, Helen (1941 [1978]), *The Consumer Movement,* New York: Harper, reprinted New York: Arno Press.

Spears, Ethel M. (1947), "The Use of Music in Industry," *Conference Board Reports: No. 78,* New York: National Industrial Conference Board.

Steglar, Carlton John (1938), "Consumer Education in the Schools: Its Immediate and Future Effect on Retailing," *Bulletin of the National Retail Dry Goods Association,* 20 (February), 63.

Stern, Aimee L. (1984), "The Teenager of the '80s: An Independent Realist," *Marketing Communications,* 9 (November), 17–9+.

Stetson, P. C. (1920), "Selling a Building Campaign," *Elementary School Journal,* 20 (March), 530–6.

Stone, Gregory P. (1954), "City Shoppers and Urban Identification: Observations on the Social Psychology of City Life," *American Journal of Sociology,* 60 (July), 36–45.

Stores (1988), "Future Shoppers: Children Today, and Tomorrow," 70 (May), 41.

————— (1989), "'Cohorts' Study: Age Matters," 71 (November), 36–7.

Strasser, Susan (1989), *Satisfaction Guaranteed: The Making of the American Mass Market,* New York: Pantheon Books.

Talbot, Constance (1937), "Ready-to-Wear," *Bulletin of the National Retail Dry Goods Association,* 20 (May), 46.

Taylor, Tom (1988), "The Transition to Adulthood in Comparative Perspective: Professional Males in Germany and the United States at the Turn of the Century," *Journal of Social History,* 21 (Summer), 634–58.

Tedlow, Richard S. (1990), *New and Improved: The Story of Mass Marketing in America,* New York: Basic Books.

Terhune, Mary [pen name, Marion Harland] (1871), "Getting on in the World," *Godey Lady's Book,* 82 (February), 135–142.

The American Experience (1989), "Mr. Sears Catalogue," transcript of National Public Television broadcast November 14, 1989, New York: Journal Graphic Transcripts.

Titus, Charles H. (1935), "The University and its Public Relations," *Journal of Higher Education,* 6 (January), 13–20+.

Townsend, A. L. (1924), "Splitting Up the Campaign's Copy Appeal to

Reach Specific Classes," *Printers' Ink,* 129 (November 13), 143–4+.

Travis, Jerome (1926), "Westinghouse 'Merchandises' Opportunity to College Men," *Printers' Ink,* 134 (February 4), 41–2.

Treece, James B. (1990), "They're Still Groping," *Business Week,* 3168 (July 9), 31.

Vance, L. J. (1896), "About College Publications," *Printers' Ink,* 16 (July 1), 21–2.

Vincent, E. (1925), "Here Comes the Bride," *New Republic,* 43 (June 17), 96–7.

Wallace, Janet (1988), "The Junior Customer: Who is She, and What Does She Want?" *Stores,* 70 (January), 53–8+.

Wallis, Dorothy L. (1959), *The Jantzen Story,* New York: Fairchild Publications.

Waples, Douglas (1934), "A Study of the Relationship between Reading Interest and Actual Reading," *The Library Quarterly,* 4 (January), 76–112.

Watkins, Julian Lewis (1949), *The 100 Greatest Advertisements: Who Wrote Them and What They Did,* New York: Moore Publishing Co.

Wentworth, Harold and Stuart B. Flexner (1967), *Dictionary of American Slang,* New York: Thomas Y. Crowell Company.

Wheeler, Joseph L. (1924), *The Library and the Community: Increased Book Service Through Library Publicity Based on Community Studies,* Chicago: American Library Association.

————— (1935), "Methods for Making Known to Inexperienced Readers the Resources and Facilities Offered by American Public Libraries," *The Library Quarterly,* 4 (October), 371–406.

Wirth, Louis (1928), *The Ghetto,* Chicago: University of Chicago Press.

White, Percival (1927), *Scientific Marketing Management: Its Principles and Methods,* New York: Harper.

Wolfe, Albert Benedict (1913), *The Lodging House Problem in Boston,* Cambridge, MA: Harvard University Press.

Wolff, Geoffrey (1990), *The Final Club,* New York: Alfred A. Knopf.

Yocum, James Carlton (1934), *Expenditures and Buying Habits of Ohio State University Students,* Ohio State University Bureau of Business Research Special Bulletin.

Yorovich, B. G. (1982), "A Game of Hide-and-Seek," *Advertising Age,* 53 (August 2), 5–7.

Zald, Mayer (1970), *Organizational Change: The Political Economy of the YMCA,* Chicago: The University of Chicago Press.

INDEX

AMERICAN
MARKETING
ASSOCIATION

YOU NEVER GET ENOUGH . . . .

As a marketing professional you'll never get enough information about marketing. The body of knowledge is being added to constantly. Success stories, and even stories of failure are written daily.

There's only one way to stay up-to-date with the latest academic theories, the "war" stories, the global techniques, and the leading technologies.

Become a member of the American Marketing Association.

For a free membership information kit;
call us at 312-648-0536
FAX us at 312-993-7542
write us at 250 S. Wacker Drive, Chicago, Illinois 60606 or contact your local AMA Chapter.

TITLES OF INTEREST IN MARKETING, DIRECT MARKETING, AND SALES PROMOTION

For further information or a current catalog, write:
NTC Business Books
a division of *NTC Publishing Group*
4255 West Touhy Avenue
Lincolnwood, Illinois 60646-1975 U.S.A.

Y